# LATIN AMERICAN THOUGHT

## PROBLEMS AND PERSPECTIVES – THREE CASE STUDIES

KAROL DERWICH

MAGDALENA MODRZEJEWSKA

# LATIN AMERICAN THOUGHT

## PROBLEMS AND PERSPECTIVES – THREE CASE STUDIES

CRACOW 2015

Reviewer
Silvana Gómez

Edition
Judyta Zegan

Cover design
Emilia Dajnowicz

Publication financed by Faculty of International
and Political Studies, Jagiellonian University in Krakow

ISBN 978-83-7638-677-5

KSIĘGARNIA AKADEMICKA
ul. św. Anny 6, 31-008 Kraków
tel./fax: 12 431-27-43, 12 663-11-67
e-mail: akademicka@akademicka.pl

Online bookstore:
www.akademicka.pl

# TABLE OF CONTENTS

# ACKNOWLEDGMENT

This book was possible thanks to generous support of the Faculty of International and Political Studies of the Jagiellonian University, Cracow, Poland. We would like to express our gratitude to all participants of both conferences organized by Doctor JustynaOlko: "Latin America and Europe. Cross-cultural Transfers and Quest for Understanding in November 2011" as well as "Crossing Boundaries Within and Beyond Academia: Responsibilities and Challenges from the Perspective of the Humanities" in October 2012 that took place at Warsaw for their insightful, critical and helpful comments. The important impulse to write this book came from the participants of Europe-Latin America Seminar organized by Professor Czeslaw Porebski. We also want to thanks our students who participated in the course "History of Latin American Thought". They were the severe and frank critics and we genuinely appreciate all their opinions.

DOI: 10.12797/9788376386775.01

# INTRODUCTION

# DOES LATIN AMERICAN PHILOSOPHY/THOUGHT EXIST?
## CULTURALISTS VERSUS UNIVERSALISTS

The intensive discussions and mature academic considerations about Latin American philosophy and Latin American thought started in the 1940s and 1950s. Surprisingly we might observe two, apparently contradictory, directions from the very beginning. On the one hand, there is an ongoing debate about the qualities and features of such a Latin American philosophy, as such, and multiple attempts to describe it in the most accurate way. While on the other hand, many thinkers would ask the most basic question: whether the Latin American philosophy or Latin American thought exists at all?[1]. Some of them would even deny its existence.

---

[1] It is worth noticing that similar discussion took place about the existence of the North American philosophy. The attempts to prove the distinctiveness of American philosophy appeared at the beginning of the 20th century, after the appearance of Pragmatism. The best example might be the book by I. W. Riley, *American Philosophy, the early schools*, New York, Dodd Mead, 1907. At the same time we can observe quite an opposite tendency. B. Kuklick in his *A History of Philosophy in America, 1720-2000*, Oxford, Clarendon Press, 2001 rather tends to report the existence of numerous European philosophical schools and currents in America (i.e. Hegelian in St Louis) than argue for the existence of distinct American philosophy. The discussion about the distinctiveness of Latin American philosophy started on in 1940s, and

The academic discussions that started in the middle of the 20th century were strongly supported by Pan-American institutions[2]. The best proof for the lack of earlier interests in Latin American philosophy can be found in the earliest edition of the *Handbook of Latin American Studies*, where philosophy as a separate discipline was not listed till 1939[3]. Numerous explanations for such a late appearance can easily be provided. As Risieri Frondizi stated, "A symptom of cultural independence that is conquering Latin America day by day is growing in quantity and quality of philosophical production. Of all human activities, philosophy is the last to appear, since it requires a cultural climate that cannot be improvised. While the technique of

---

continued. See: R. Frondizi, *Is There an Ibero-American Philosophy?*, "Philosophy and Phenomenological Research" III 1949, Vol. 9, No. 3, Special Issue – Second Inter-American Congress of Philosophy, pp. 345-355; L. Zea, *Philosophy and Thought in Latin America*, "Latin American Research Review" 1968, Vol. 3, No. 2 (Spring), pp. 3-16; O. R. Marti, *Is There a Latin American Philosophy*, "Metaphilosophy" 1983, Vol. 14, No. 1, pp. 46-52; J. J. E. Gracia, *Latin American Philosophy in the Twentieth Century*, Buffalo, Prometheus Books, 1986; L. Zea, *Identity: A Latin American Philosophical Problem*, "Philosophical Forum" 1988/1989, Vol. 20, No. 1-2 (Fall-Winter), pp. 33-42; S. Nuccetelli, *Is "Latin-American Thought" Philosophy*, "Methaphilosophy" 2003, Vol. 34, No. 4 (July), pp. 524-536; W. Redmont, *Self-awareness in Latin-American Colonial Philosophy*, Part 1, "Jahrbuch für Geschichte Lateinamerikas" 2004, No. 41, pp. 353-372 and Part 2, "Jahrbuch für Geschichte Lateinamerikas" 2005, No. 42, pp. 209-234.

[2] The majority of the research was supported, at the time, by the action within the Pan-American movement, either by the Pan American Union Division of Intellectual Cooperation or by the First Inter American Conference (Primera Conferencia Interamericana de Filosofía) which was held at Yale in 1943, by the First Inter American Congress of Philosophy (Primero Congreso Interamericano de Filosofía) that was held in 1944 in Haiti, and by the Inter American Congress of Philosophy (Segundo Congreso Interamericano de Filosofía) that was held in New York at Columbia University in 1947. Cf. C. Krusé, *The Third Inter-American Congress of Philosophy*, "The Journal of Philosophy" 1950, Vol. 47, No. 12, pp. 364-366.

[3] Even currently, some compendia pertinent to Latin America disregard philosophy. Cf. Ph. Swanson, *The Companion to Latin American Studies*, London, Arnold, 2003.

any nature whatsoever, can be assimilated quickly even by illiterate people, philosophy – and with it, all the higher manifestations of the spirit – tub requires a spiritual maturity that is the result of slow cultural training"[4].

At the same time as we observe this quest, a group of Latin American philosophers conducted an extensive debate about whether the authentic Latin American philosophy exists. The voices of denial were quite common, even though those thinkers that were responsible for the initiation of such a debate, and mainly contributed to it, were aware of the short and vague tradition of philosophic inquiry in Latin America. In 1940, Risieri Frondizi wrote: "There is no Latin American philosophy in the sense we give to the term when we speak of a British philosophy, or of a German or French and Italian, or modern and contemporary, or North American philosophy beginning with Peirce, Royce, and James. In other words, there has not been any original philosophy in Latin America which may be the genuine expression of the spiritual characteristics of Latin Americans. The so-called Latin American philosophy is nothing more than the reformulation of philosophical problems which originated in Europe. Hence, to be concerned about its history is to deal with the influence that European philosophy had on it"[5]. In 1949, in his

---

[4] "Un síntoma de la independencia cultural que conquista día a día la América Latina es el crecimiento, en cantidad y en calidad, de la producción filosófica. De todas las actividades humanas, la filosofía es la última en aparecer, pues supone un clima cultular que no puede improvisarse. Mientras que la técnica, de cualquier naturaleza que sea, puede ser asimilada rápidamente aun por pueblos incultos, la filosofía – y con ella todas las manifestaciones superiores del espíritu – exige tina madurez espiritual que es el resultado de una lenta formación cultural. Por otra parte, exige también un clima de libertad que las vicisitudes de la formación política de las naciones latinoamericanas impidieron que se alcanzara en el siglo pasado". R. Frondizi, *Philosophy*, "Handbook of Latin American Studies" 1939, Vol. 6, p. 418.

[5] Idem, *Panorama de la filosofia latinoamericana contemporanea*, "Minerva" 1944, Vol. 1, No. 2, p. 95. Quoted by and in translation of J. J. E. Gracia, *Philosophy and*

Spanish *La filosofía latinoamericana contemporánea* Anibal Sanchez Reulet also paid attention to impossibility to apply such "European norms" and "if, when say 'philosophy', we think only of the great figures of European thought in the three or four countries where philosophic activity was at its highest, it is obvious that Latin American philosophy cannot sustain the comparison. And the answer will be in the negative. But it is unjust to pose the problem on this plane". Then Reulet continues his argument, proving, that "[t]he fact that Latin American philosophy has not reached the same level does not invalidate the importance of the effort made. Nor the intrinsic value of its results"[6].

The debate was led by two groups, which later on came to be known as the culturalists and the universalists. The culturalists were convinced that due to cultural context characteristic, distinct Latin American thought or Latin American philosophy exists. The most prominent supporter of the culturalist approach would be Leopoldo Zea who maintained that the claims are always contextual, rooted in a cultural tradition which will determine thinkers' perspective[7]. Universalists argue that the methods and problems of philosophy are universal, that the methods of philosophy are similar to those in science and therefore, one cannot talk about Latin American

---

*Literature in Latin America*, New York, State University of New York Press, 1989.

[6] A. Sánchez Reulet, *Contemporary Latin-American Philosophy: A Selection, with an Introduction and Notes*, Albuquerque, University of New Mexico Press, 1954, p. XIX. The publication was translated into English in 1954 and we used English edition.

[7] L. Zea, *The Actual Function of Philosophy in Latin America*, [in:] J. J. E Gracia, E. Millán-Zaibert, *Latin American Philosophy for the 21st Century: The Human Condition, Values, and the Search for Identity*, Amherst, New York, Prometheus Books, 2004, pp. 401-413; S. Nuccetelli, *Latin American Thought: Philosophical Problems and Arguments*, Boulder, Colorado, Westview Press, 2002, pp. 243-246.

philosophy[8]. One of the major proponents of the Universalist approach was Risieri Frondizi, already mentioned.

Jorge J. E. Gracia pointed out that apart from the traditionally recognized culturalist/universalist debate, we should identify two additional approaches. The first one was the critical approach that was formulated by Augusto Salazar Bondy. He recognized the close relation between philosophy and social conditions[9]. According to him, the conditions existing in the area preclude the development of philosophy, because all the philosophy developed by Latin Americans is inauthentic and therefore not true philosophy. The dependence of Latin America on ideas imported from elsewhere, or its situation as dominated, prevents it from being authentic; it is a borrowed, subservient philosophy"[10].

Gracia made a very important observation (that was already mentioned by Reulet), that all these positions are based on "pre-established conceptions of philosophy that de-legitimize others. The issue, then, does not have to do with Latin American philosophy as such, but with the nature of philosophy"[11]. Therefore, Gracia tries to answer this fundamental question and proposed the concept of an ethnic philosophy. According to him "An ethnic philosophy is the philosophy of an ethnos. This requires both the existence of the ethnos and a certain conception of philosophy by the ethnos. The ethnos, just as its philosophy, is not conceived in essentialist

---

[8]  G. Yancy, *Philosophy in Multiple Voices*, Lanham, Rowman & Littlefield Publishers, 2007, pp. 191-192; J. J. E. Gracia, *Philosophy and Its History: Issues in Philosophical Historiography*, Albany, State University of New York Press, 1992, pp. 158-167.

[9]  A. Salazar Bondy, *The Meaning and Problem of Hispanic American Thought*, Lawrence, Center of Latin American Studies of the University of Kansas, 1969.

[10]  J. J. E. Gracia, *Identity and Latin American Philosophy*, [in:] S. Nuccetelli, O. Schutte, O. Bue, *A Companion to Latin American Philosophy*, Malden, Massachusetts, Wiley-Blackwell, 2010, p. 259.

[11]  *Ibidem.*

terms; there is no need for the ethnos or its philosophy to have a set of properties that are constant throughout their existence. Ethne are conceived in familial-historical terms; they are groups of people who have been brought together by history"[12]. Therefore, for Gracia "This means that, just as the ethnos that produces it, Latin American philosophy need not have essential characteristics that, first, are shared by everything considered to be part of Latin American philosophy and, second, separate it from all other philosophies. It is only necessary that Latin American philosophy be whatever the historical circumstances that originated it and the ethnos that produced it made it. Because the unity of Latin American philosophy is historical and contextual, it becomes easier to account for its variety and for the inclusion in it of texts and figures that traditional Western philosophy might not consider philosophical, such as the *Popol Vuh* or the poems of Sor Juana. The criteria for inclusion are historical and contextual, and open to change and development"[13].

Also, Manuel Varga is trying to prove that it is barely possible to find the unifying element: "I am skeptical that there is anything interesting that unifies the various things that might appropriately be labeled «Latin American philosophy». Instead, what I mean to refer to by «the nature of Latin American philosophy» is a motley, a variegated cluster of nonessential, contingently-had characteristics within a diverse set of philosophical discourses and practices that are, nevertheless, widespread within the philosophical networks in Latin America and present in the philosophy produced by those networks"[14].

---

[12] *Ibidem*, p. 260. Cf. J. J. E. Gracia, *Race, Ethnicity, and Nationality: A Challenge for the 21st Century*, Lanham, Maryland, Rowman & Littlefield, 2005.

[13] *Ibidem*, p. 260. Cf. J. J. E. Gracia, *What is Latin American Philosophy?*, [in:] G. Yancy, *op. cit.*

[14] M. Vargas, *"Real" Philosophy, Metaphilosophy and Metametaphilosophy: On the Plight of Latin*, "CR: The New Centennial Review" 2007, Vol. 7, No. 3 (Winter), p. 52.

Taking all the disputes among Latin American thinkers and how much efforts they dedicated to prove or deny the existence of Latin American philosophy and Latin American thought into account, it might be stated that all those doubts are the best proof for such an existence. That is the reason why Edgar Montiel suggested that we should apply Descartes' paradox "The appropriate response to this question is: 'It doubts therefore it exists'"[15]. Implementing this approach, we cannot deny the existence of Latin America philosophy and Latin American thought.

# FILLING THE GAP

In the last few decades, we have observed a rapid increase of interest in Latin American philosophy and Latin American thought. However, as Susana Nuccetelli correctly pointed out: "students, teachers, and other scholars who seek to learn about Latin American thought currently find an obstacle in the lack of adequate materials. Original sources, if not completely unknown, are often difficult to obtain"[16]. There are numerous reasons for the lack of sufficient literature, among them those mentioned by Nuccetelli. But the most important one seems to be different. Latin American thought has arisen as the result of culturalist aspirations and claims about the cultural uniqueness of Latin America, leading to their intellectual distinctiveness. However, as Manuel Varga pointed out "there are not many philosophers in the 'analytic' core of the profession who make it their task to write about nature, status, and the direction of culture. What works there tends to be about the implications of culture, its social construction and its effects. Practically nothing is done at the level

---

[15] E. Montiel, *Three Decisive Battles for Latin American Philosophy*, "Cultura: New Dimensions of Music, Literature and Philosophy" 1982, Vol. 8, No. 2.
[16] S. Nuccetelli, *Latin American Thought...*, p. XIV.

of offering a fundamental ontology of culture. There are a number of reasons why this might be so. Perhaps there is a sense that culture is too amorphous for a serious, rigorous philosophical reflection. Perhaps many philosophers simply prefer to avoid running the risks that are endemic to reflection on culture. Philosophical writing on cultural differences has been plagued by an unflattering collection of vices—racism, sexism, Eurocentrism, and so on—so, maybe we are better off passing over these topics in silence"[17].

Starting from the mid-20th century, the first comprehensive studies dedicated to Latin American thought and philosophy began to appear. It is worth mentioning some of the most esteemed publications pertinent to Latin American philosophy and thought: the classical and the first comprehensive analysis *Pensamiento latinoamericano* by Leopoldo Zea, *¿Existe una filosofía de nuestra América?* by Augusto Salazar Bondy (1968). *A Century of Latin American Thought* by William Crawford (1961); *Latin American Thought: A Historical Introduction* by Harold Davis (1972); *Cultural Identity and Social Liberation in Latin American Thought* by Ofelia Schutte (1993); *Latin American Thought: Philosophical Problems and Arguments* by Susana Nuccetelli (2002); *Latin American Philosophy: Currents, Issues, Debates* edited by Eduardo Mendieta (2003); *El pensamiento filosofico latinoamericano, del Caribe y "latino" (1300-2000): historia, corrientes, temas y filósofos* edited by Enrique Dussel, Eduardo Mendieta, and Carmen Bohórquez (2009); last but not least we should mentioned opulent *A Companion to Latin American Philosophy* edited by Susana Nuccetelli, Ofelia Schutte, and Otávio Bueno (2010). *Philosophy and Literature in Latin America: A Critical Assessment of the Current Situation* by Jorge J. E. Gracia (1989)

---

[17] M. Varga, *On the Value of Philosophy: The Latin American Case*, "Comparative Philosophy" 2010, Vol. 1, No. 1, p. 33. Varga made his claim about philosophy's culture of silence about culture and lack of interests among North American philosophers, but we believe its applicable also in a broader sense, toward the Western word.

and *El pensamiento latinoamericano y su aventura* by Arturo Andrés Roig (1994).

There is a growing body of anthology of primary sources, including: *Latin American Philosophy: An Introduction with Readings* by Susana Nuccetelli and Gary Seay (2003) and *Latin American Philosophy for the 21st Century: The Human Condition, Values, and the Search for Identity* by Jorge J. E. Gracia and Elizabeth Millán-Zaibert (2004).

It is also worth mentioning the writings dedicated to a more narrowed analysis, such as: *The Identity of Liberation in Latin American Thought: Latin American Historicism and the Phenomenology of Leopoldo Zea* by Mario Sáenz (1999).

Even though, as we pointed out, there is a substantial body of literature, the academic dialogue about the existence of Latin American philosophy and attempts to provide deep and broad analyses seems to be insufficient. Susana Nuccetelli made very thoughtful and observant remarks, something that she labeled as an "invisibility" problem. "Latin American philosophy is invisible because it faces:

- An Internal Dialogue Problem (IDP): There is no (stable) philosophical dialogue among Latin American philosophers, and
- An External Dialogue Problem (EDP): There is no (stable, reciprocal) philosophical dialogue between Latin American philosophers and their Western peers[18].

---

[18] This point of view Susana Nuccetelli called the "new skepticism". According to her it is shared by authors like Maite Ezcurdia, Eduardo García-Ramírez, Guillermo Hurtado, Carlos Pereda and Eduardo Rabossi. Those labeled by her as "new skeptics" claimed that "Latin American philosophy lacks inner and outer dialogue of the sort needed to develop stable philosophical traditions and communities". Cf. M. Ezcurdia, *Originalidad y presencia*, [in:] J. C. Cruz Revueltas, *La filosofía en América Latina como problema y un epílogo desde la otra orilla*, Mexico City, Publicaciones Cruz, 2003, pp. 196-202; E. García-Ramírez, *On the Invisibility Problem of Latin*

The accusation made by skeptics about the lack of both: internal and external dialogue seems to be quite right. When we overview the literature related to Latin American thought and philosophy, it seems to be reduced toward particularities and a lack of this external dialogue. In most of the cases, we have found edited compilation of collected papers, however, due to the limited form of our book, our analyses are also quite narrow and fragmented. Scholars do not seek to find and present the common features existing on the continental, Latin American level, but rather attempt to display the narrowly defined phenomena, limiting their analysis to one country. This lack of internal dialogue seems to be a common feature of "Third World scholars"[19].

We do not have pretentious aspirations to fill this gap. We just hope to provide a humble chronicle of existing literature, create some form of a map, reveal blind spots, and popular interests. We also intend to trace methods and paradigms in the research about Latin American thought, and reveal its multidisciplinary,

American Philosophy, "APA Newsletter on Hispanic/Latino Issues in Philosophy" 2011, Vol. 10, No. 2 (Spring), pp. 12-17, http://c.ymcdn.com/sites/www.apaon line. org/resource/collection/60044C96-F3E0-4049-BC5A-271C673FA1E5/v10n2 Hispanic.pdf; G. Hurtado, Two Models of Latin American Philosophy, "Journal of Speculative Philosophy" 2006, Vol. 20, No. 3, pp. 204-213; G. Hurtado, El búho y la serpiente. Ensayos sobre la filosofía en México en el siglo XX, Mexico City, UNAM, 2007; C. Pereda, Latin American Philosophy: Some Vices, "Journal of Speculative Philosophy" 2006, Vol. 20, No. 3, pp. 192-203; E. Rabossi, Filosofar. Profesionalismo, profesionalidad, tics y modales, [in:] J. C. Cruz Revueltas (ed.), op. cit., pp. 34-44; E. Rabossi, En el comienzo Dios creo el Canon. Biblia berolinensis. Ensayos sobre la condición de la filosofía, Buenos Aires, Gedisa, 2008 (especially chapter El canon); see also S. Nuccetelli, Latin American Philosophy: Metaphilosophical Foundations, [in:] The Stanford Encyclopedia of Philosophy (Summer 2014 Edition), E. N. Zalta (ed.), http://plato.stanford.edu/archives/sum2014/entries/latin-american-metaphilosophy/ (01.09.2015).

[19] P. J. Hountondji, Scientific Dependence in Africa Today, "Research in African Literatures" 1990, Vol. 21, No. 3, pp. 5-15.

interdisciplinary or transdisciplinary methodology. In the last few decades, we observed numerous debates regarding [the following] serious questions: Whether Latin American thought exists as a separate and distinct thought from European/North American or Asian thought? To what extent are these cultural-geographic criteria applicable to create such a typology in the fields pertinent to thought or philosophy? Is it more appropriate to talk about the existence of Latin American thought or Latin American philosophy in Latin America? The term thought has a broader sense. These questions illustrate the meta-question and the dispute between the universalists and culturalists. They also reflect the great need for recognition of deep, rich and long intellectual tradition in Latin America. One of the essential inquiries touches upon the considerations about the imitation of Western thought and Latin American innovation, about the quest for identity, and mirroring, about the returning the gaze, and mutuality. In the upcoming three essays we want to touch these questions, first looking at the methods and paradigms in the research on Latin American thought, then look at the cases of positivism that might be valid proof of innovative adaptation and we decided to dedicate the last essay to anarchism, which might provide arguments for the aforementioned imitation in Latin American thought.

## WHAT'S IN A NAME – THOUGHT OR PHILOSOPHY?

Even the question whether we should adopt the name "philosophy" or the name "thought" to describe the intellectual activities in Latin America in the most accurate way is difficult to determine. We decided to use the notion "Latin American thought" rather than Latin American philosophy for various reasons:

The term "Latin American thought" allows for the better accommodation of the broad spectrum of intellectual activities that can find their expression in literature, religion or art. It also seems to be the most accurate equivalent of the Spanish notion "pensamiento";

The term "philosophy" seems to be built on the deeply European or Western understanding of this notion, therefore applying it to non-Western intellectual tradition seems to be biased, and such a strict and narrow perception and interpretation reveals strong eurocentricity.

By using the term "Latin American thought" it would be possible to accommodate the thinkers that created works that contain philosophical elements, but are not pure philosophy (created and motivated by the love of wisdom)[20].

There are multiple voices claiming that one of the specifics and distinctive elements of Latin American philosophical inquiry is its unphilosophical nature, in terms of the form in which it express itself. For that reason, philosophical examinations are performed within the domain of history, religion or literature. As Antonio Caso argues "The history of philosophy is usually written in the exclusive sense of the history of the systems. This is a serious error. Philosophical systems do not represent all philosophy, not even all systematic philosophy. The philosophical ideas revise a much broader spectrum: poetic, historical, political, religious, ones that have not been formulated in strictly systematic statements"[21]. Therefore, he

---

[20] As Nuccetelli framed this common postulate: "A theory is philosophical (in the strict sense) if and only if it sets forth philosophical problems motivated by philosophical interests". Cf. S. Nuccetelli, *Is "Latin American Thought...*, p. 531.

[21] "La Historia de la Filosofía se ha escrito generalmente en el sentido exclusive de la historia de los sistemas. Este es un grave error. Los sistemas filosóficos no son toda la filosofía, ni siquiera toda la filosofía sistemática. Las ideas filosóficas revisten foro mas poéticas, históricas, políticas, religiosas, que no se formularon en enunciados rig-

also believed that "The philosophical activity is not something in-dependent from life and action, from Art and Science"[22].

Another problem is the Eurocentric definitions of philosophy, that are made from the Western perspective. Fred Gillette Sturm rightly pointed out: "Definitions of 'philosophy' are based too fre-quently on the prejudices of cultural context or on the platform of some new intellectual movement. For years Europeans have claimed the world for their own, insisting that philosophy is a uniquely oc-cidental phenomenon with roots exclusively in classical Greek cul-ture, with no counterpart in Asia, Africa, or the Americas except where Europeanization of thought has occurred. Within European philosophical history, adherents of new movements have issued manifestos seeking to exempt older Intellectual movements from the designation, insisting that there is only one legitimate problem-atic for philosophic thought, namely theirs, and only one legitimate methodology for doing philosophy, namely theirs"[23].

So even though, some writers try to solve this Gordian knot by redefining the term philosophy and use it in the broader sense, it might be unconvincing. Sturm decided to use the term "Philoso-phy" as "broad enough to include all areas of thought which have been designated 'philosophic' in the intellectual history of human cultures. Philosophy is the effort to satisfy human concern with questions of meaning and order"[24]. Nevertheless, still such an al-teration might be insufficient, hence the demand for better, more precise framing might lead to the labeling and exclusion of the vast

---

urosamente sistemáticos". A. Caso, *Filósofos y doctrinas morales*, Mexico City, Porrúa Hermanos, 1915, p. 11.

[22] "La actividad filosófica no es algo independiente de la vida y de la acción, del Arte y la Ciencia", *ibidem*, p. 12.

[23] F. G. Sturm, *Dependence and Originality in Iberoamerican Philosophy*, "Interna-tional Philosophical Quarterly", Vol. 20, No. 3, pp. 256-257.

[24] *Ibidem*, p. 257.

intellectual heritage, which would not be able to fit into westernized standards.

Applying the notion of Latin American thought also allows to include those works that were not motivated by the pure need for intellectual speculation, but were created and motivated by social or political reason. As Risieri Frondizi stated: "It is undeniable that the works of Sarmiento, Bello, or Martí – to mention three great examples – contain philosophical ideas. But such ideas appear as a result of literary or political concerns to which they remain subordinated. In none of them does philosophy have an independent status; none of them set forth philosophical problems motivated by philosophical interests"[25].

Susana Nuccetelli avoids the dilemma either to use notion thought or philosophy by creating the distinction within the notion of philosophy. She is trying to separate the philosophy in an academic sense from the non-academic type of philosophy. The first one: "Academic philosophy, or *autonomous philosophy as practiced in the West since the Enlightenment*, did not begin in Latin America until the first half of the twentieth century"[26]. The "non-academic type of philosophy consistently prospered in Latin America from the sixteenth century to the present. It comprises philosophical positions expressed in essay format, a hybrid genre cultivated by political and religious leaders, scientists, and literary figures, who, interested in the intersection of philosophy with literature, religion, and politics, arguably made contributions to the intellectual history of Latin America. As may be expected, however, the line separating academic and non-academic philosophy is not always sharp"[27].

---

[25] R. Frondizi, *Is There an Ibero-American...*, p. 346.
[26] S. Nuccetelli, *Latin American Philosophy....*
[27] *Ibidem.*

Ofelia Schutte paid attention to the "Latin American tradition of *pensamiento*, literary political and philosophical thought articulated primarily in essay form"[28].

## GEOGRAPHIC BOUNDARIES VERSUS CULTURAL BOUNDARIES

When we talk about the Latin American philosophy, the main distinctions seem to be drawn based on geographic boundaries, and the subject of our considerations will be pertinent to Latin America as the continent. However, even such simple solution seems to be problematic. It is hard to draw such sharp continental boundaries. There is no unanimity about the notion of Latin America. To focus on some principal issues and tendencies in Latin American thought, it is necessary to define what is meant when the common phrase "Latin America" is used. This is of great importance as it can have a significant impact on the nature of Latin American thought, and – most importantly – it is of fundamental meaning for the debate on the identity of the region today called Latin America and its citizens. It is also important to define the term "Latin America" because of its young history. The term has commonly been used since the mid-20th century. It was popularized by the creation of the United Nations Economic Commission for Latin America and the Caribbean (Spanish: Comisión Económica para America Latina y el Caribe – CEPAL). However, the term appeared for the first time in the mid-19th century in France. There are opinions that it could be created by famous Chilean thinker, Andrés Bello. Earlier, in the colonial period and in the early 19th century this region was described as the New World, West Indies, Indies, or just America. In the 19th century, there

---

[28] O. Schutte, *Cultural Identity and Social Liberation in Latin American Thought*, Albany, State University of New York Press, 1993, p. 4.

was a popular tendency to contrast South and Central America and the Caribbean region to the Anglo-Saxon North America. It is not a coincidence that the term appeared in France which, at that time, was the center of European intellectual life and had growing political and intellectual aspirations. Reference to the Latin heritage was much broader than just the underlying Hispanic or Iberian tradition of the region. It is justified as France has its colonies in the region but the French contribution – until that period – was incomparably smaller than Spanish and Portuguese. That is why the terms Hispanoamerica or Iberoamerica – that also appeared in the second half of the 19th century were more popular until the 1940s. Today "Latin America" is understood as the region from the Rio Grande river in the north to the Tierra del Fuego and Cape Horn in the south. As the geopolitical circumstances of the Latin component of the Western Hemisphere are changing, it produces great challenges to the present Latin American thought. There are former British colonies in the geographical frontiers of Latin America. There is also a huge Latin American community in the United States where regions Latinized to a great extent are present. Today the term "Latin America" is much more complicated than just the opposition to the Anglo-Saxon America. It is much more multidimensional[29]. This ultra-complicated nature of Latin America produces very important discussion related to the identity of the region and its citizens.

Another alternative is to use cultural boundaries; as Pablo Iannone pointed out in his *Latin American Philosophy*: "Philosophers sometimes speak of Ibero-American philosophy, meaning philosophy practiced or philosophical ideas and concerns found in predominantly Spanish- or Portuguese-speaking countries of Europe and the Americas. Hispanic philosophy is subsumed under Ibero-American philosophy, being philosophy practiced or philosophical

---

[29] A. Dembicz, *Filozofia poznawania Ameryki*, Warsaw, CESLA, 2010, pp. 17-34.

ideas and concerns found in predominantly Spanish-speaking countries of Europe and the Americas. Latin American philosophy overlaps with the previous two categories, being philosophy practiced or philosophical ideas and concerns found in countries of the Americas other than the United States and Canada, whether their predominant language is Spanish as in many of them, Portuguese as in Brazil, or Guaraní (together with Spanish) as in Paraguay. In short, the term Latin American philosophy applies to Western-influenced philosophy and philosophies developed since the Conquest that are typically – though not necessarily always – formulated in Spanish or Portuguese"[30].

When we take these cultural boundaries into consideration, then some parts that are distinct both: culturally and linguistically, even though geographically are located in Latin America, cannot be considered as a part of the Latin American philosophical heritage. The best example would be the case of "Guyana (whose predominant languages are English and East Indian), Surinam (where Dutch is predominant), and French Guyana (where the predominant language is French) are geographically part of Latin America, not many consider them to be part of Latin America from a cultural or philosophical standpoint"[31].

Therefore, as Nuccetelli pointed out "Latin American philosophers have expressed a number of different preferences about what to call the field. The standard name preferred here has been 'Latin American philosophy'. But there are other options, depending on whether 'thought' takes the place of 'philosophy', and/or 'Iberoamerican', 'Hispanic', 'Hispanic-American' or 'Latino/a' (among other qualifiers) takes the place of 'Latin American'. (…) There is no common rationale for substituting any of the above qualifiers for 'Latin

---

[30]  P. I a n n o n e (ed.), *Latin American Philosophy*, [in:] i d e m, *Dictionary of World Philosophy*, New York, Routledge, 2001, p. 301.

[31]  *Ibidem*, p. 301.

American". But each proposed qualifier (including 'Latin American') inherits a problem faced by the proper name from which it derives"[32].

The solution offered by Jorge Gracia is to provide instead of definition what Latin American means in "negative" term, framing definition by exclusion: *Latin American* refers to everything in the Americas that is not American (U. S.) or Canadian, even if strictly speaking it should include the French parts of Canada. Indeed, sometimes it even excludes those parts of the Caribbean and South America that were French, Dutch, or English colonies, such as Haiti and Jamaica[33].

Different attempts, mentioned by Nuccetelli, were made by Eduardo Rabossi who provides a set of criteria (both sufficient and necessary) to be called "Latin America". He refers to countries of North, Central, and South America by virtue of their sharing "a common political origin (Spanish/Portuguese conquest), a similar linguistic heritage (Spanish/Portuguese), a dominant religion (Catholicism), and comparable predicaments *vis à vis* local, regional, and international affairs"[34] be as Nuccetelli pointed out "Rabossi's criteria, which

---

[32] S. Nuccetelli, *Latin American Philosophy: Metapsychical Foundation.*

[33] J. J. E. Gracia, *Forging People: Race, Ethnicity and Nationality in Hispanic American and Latino/a Thought,* Notre Dame, Indiana, University of Notre Dame Press, 2011, p. 8. At the same time Gracia tries to define Iberoamerican by explaining who they are, not by telling who they are not: "The category 'Hispanic' may be understood broadly to include the categories 'Spanish', 'Spanish American', 'Iberian', 'Iberoamerican', 'Latin American', and 'Latino/a'. 'Iberian' has to do with Spain or Portugal. 'Iberoamerican' refers to the parts of the Americas that were conquered by Spain and Portugal and stayed under their control", *ibidem*.

[34] E. Rabossi, *Latin American Philosophy*, [in:] Th. Baldwin (ed.), *The Cambridge History of Philosophy 1870-1945*, Cambridge, Cambridge University Press, 2003, p. 507. Cf. S. Nuccetelli, *Latin American Philosophy....*

are more restrictive, avoid being too broad, but face the problem of being too narrow, which makes them unsatisfactory"[35].

As Nuccetelli noticed, Hurtado tried by this definition "to denote a culturally specific region of the Americas, one individuated by appeal to language. (…) In any case, his account of 'Latin America' and 'the Latin American' appears to point to a pragmatic problem arising from some facts about those terms' introduction into public discourse. According to Hurtado, there is historical evidence that they were introduced into public discourse in the late nineteenth century by the French, who did so in order to advance their national interest in dealing with the Latin and Catholic nations of the Americas. (…) Once these terms had caught on in thought and language, their role in discourse was unaffected by the defeat of the French in the region (…) however, Hurtado continues to use these terms without explaining why we should do so, given that, according to his own story, they were introduced for colonialist purposes—and therefore face the pragmatic problem. In addition, given this account, it would seems that those terms now refer to nothing objective at all"[36].

"[Latin America] includes countries where the Spanish, Portuguese or French language currently dominates, leaving out the countries where English and Dutch are spoken (Québec is not included because it is the region of a predominantly Anglo-Saxon country). This way of drawing the borders of the region meets an old ideological project and, ultimately, a political one. The term "Latin America" was used in the 19th century to make the argument that France had the historic mission of defending the American countries of Latin and Catholic heritage against the American countries of the Protestant and Saxon heritage. (…) Although this project collapsed forever with the withdrawal of French troops from Mexico, the Latin

---

[35]  *Ibidem.*
[36]  *Ibidem.*

American concept has been preserved since then in the imagination of the region (though not without some criticism from various political and philosophical sides)"[37].

Also replacing Latin American by 'Iberoamerican' and 'Hispanic American' would not solve the problem, then we will just struggle with the need to define 'Iberia' and 'Hispania'. "Each of these ancient proper names designates the European peninsula today divided into Spain and Portugal. Thus, taken literally, each has connotations unacceptable to the descendants of the victims of these countries' colonial policies in the Americas"[38].

---

[37] "A[merica] L[atina] comprende los países del continente en los que actualmente se habla de manera predominante el español, el portugués o el francés, dejando fuera a los países en los que se hablan el inglés y el holandés (Québec no está incluida por tratarse de la región de un país mayoritariamente anglo-sajón). Esta manera de trazar las fronteras de la región responde a un viejo proyecto ideológico y, a fin de cuentas, político. El término 'América Latina' fue utilizado en el siglo XIX para formular la tesis de que Francia tenía la misión histórica de defender a los países americanos de forja latina y católica de los países americanos de forja protestante y sajona. (…) Aunque este proyecto se derrumbó para siempre con la retirada de las tropas francesas de México, el concepto de lo latinoamericano se ha preservado desde entonces en el imaginario de la región (aunque no sin algunas críticas desde distintos flancos políticos y filosóficos). G. Hurtado, *El diálogo filosófico interamericano como un diálogo para la democracia*, "Inter-American Journal of Philosophy" 2010, Vol. 1, No. 1, p. 11.

[38] S. Nuccetelli, *Latin American Philosophy.…* Another option was offered by Gracia. For him "'Hispanic philosophy' and 'Latino/a philosophy' are more recent terms whose semantic features are not yet fully settled by usage. 'Hispanic philosophy' may roughly include Iberian philosophy as well (Gracia 2000), while 'Latino/a philosophy' is the philosophy of or about the descendants of Latin Americans abroad, especially in the United States (Gracia 2011b). As noted above in the cases of 'Iberoamerican' and 'Hispanic American', both 'Hispanic' and 'Latino/a' also appear to have inherited the pragmatic problem for the proper nouns from which each derives (it should now be obvious to the reader what those problems are)", S. Nuccetelli, *Latin American Philosophy: Metapsychical Foundation.*

DOI: 10.12797/9788376386775.02

# I. METHODS AND PARADIGMS IN LATIN AMERICAN THOUGHT

As the aim of the paper is to present the main methods and paradigms in Latin American thought it is also necessary to define what is meant by it. Is it a reflection over Latin America or is it a general reflection implemented by Latin Americans? Is it the voice of Latin Americans related to Latin American problems or even something else? As the history of the New World – to use this old description of the region – is relatively young, it is, however, quite complicated. It has its reflection in the nature of Latin American thought. As the first three centuries after the encounter of the Old and New World were determined by the building and then functioning of the colonial empires of Spain and Portugal, the only ones that can be called "Latin American thought" are the European considerations over the New World and its inhabitants. This is why until the beginning of the 19th century the only debates, discussions and considerations over the subject that is now called Latin America were restricted almost exclusively to European philosophers. It was the result of perceiving indigenous population of Latin America as an object, not a subject. The totally Eurocentric or more precisely – the Iberocentric point of view completely dominated any considerations related to the New World. After the initial encounter and during the creation of colonial empires in the New World, new questions of both an epistemological and ethical nature emerged in

Europe – especially in the Iberian Peninsula. The existence of new continent and the functioning of highly developed cultures of the Mayas, Aztecs, and Incas constituted a real shock for 19th century Europeans. The first great debate regarded the indigenous people of America – "the new man" so different, so strange, so problematic for Eurocentric conquistadors and their principals. Barbarians? Of course, yet not Christian. Human? Not sure, they are so different. Vassals? Could be, if they are barbarians, aliens, and maybe even not humans why they could not be slaves? However strange those phrases sound today, they constituted an important part of thought related to present-day Latin America. Taking its radically Eurocentric nature into account, it seems entitled to call it Latin American thought as it was an almost unique reflection on Latin American affairs of the early colonial period. It can be named a part of cultural imperialism but also, today, it constitutes an important part of Latin American thought. A thought that was emerging in the conditions of conflict between two worlds. Principally a religious conflict. According to European conquistadors, kings, catholic hierarchs and philosophers, the key element of the encounter was religion. The Christianization of infidels was their first obligation. It was the aim but also the justification of their expeditions. In the official nomenclature, Christianization was the first and often unique goal of building colonial empires. Simultaneously, because the indigenous peoples were not Christians, for a majority of Europeans, it was enough to treat them as in human or a worse kind of human. Juan Ginés Sepúlveda, Spanish philosopher, and clergyman is inscribed in that trend of interpreting the New World and its inhabitants. According to him, the conquest of the New World was justified. He thought the same about the enslavement of Indians. To Sepúlveda, the Indians were not humans. He came to that conclusion analyzing their ways of life. For him – but not only for him – they were barbarians in their nature and that was enough to deprive them of all rights that were ascribed to a man of that time. He used the same doctrine of natural slaves that Aristotle used for his argumentation. According to this doctrine, some people are natural slaves of others whose nature is more civilized. He took some principal characteristics of an indigenous group and judging them as barbarian justified their natural enslavement. Sepúlveda also used the argument that Indians are irrational beings. He argued that Indians do not have culture, written laws, and history which means that they are not rational beings[39]. Describing Indians as barbarians was a key argument of Sepúlveda and some others 16th century philosophers for justifying the war against indigenous people and their enslavement[40].

Despite the fact that, Sepúlveda's argumentation was very comfortable for the Spanish authorities, he never gained their major attention. The conquest and later creation of a colonial empire – founded on the total marginalization of the indigenous population of the New World and their enslavement and later vassalization – in fact, was the exemplification of Sepúlveda's concept. Officially, though, the Spanish court was seriously preoccupied with the resolution of the Indian "question". The official resolution was founded on the argumentation of another Spanish clergyman, Bartolomé de las Casas. Contrary to Sepúlveda, las Casas had a great personal experience in contacts with the New World and its inhabitants. The main argument used for justifying the conquest of Indians was that they were not Christians. Las Casas proved that they can be converted to Catholicism. He advocated that they were people too and, therefore, had natural rights to life and personal liberty. He insisted that the only way of Christianization was acting through peace and explanation. The principal difference between him and Sepulveda is that for las Casas, Indians were rational beings. He rejected

---

[39] J. Santos Herceg, *Filosofía de (para) la Conquista. Eurocentrismo y colonialismo en la disputa por el Nuevo Mundo*, "Atenea (Concepción)" 2011, No. 503, pp. 169-170.
[40] S. Nuccetelli, *Latin American Thought...*, p. 104.

arguments about barbarian practices of the New World's inhabitants. He admitted that some of the groups practice human sacrifice, but explained that as they were devoted believers, they offered their gods the best they had – human life.

Similarly to Bartolomé de las Casas, the Thomistic doctrine was also the base for philosophical considerations of another Dominican clergyman and philosopher, Francisco Vitoria. He tried to explain the right of Spanish authorities to conquest the New World and its inhabitants on the ground of the natural law theory. He explained that the human nature is to be rational. Every human being tries to achieve that natural state from birth and continuing throughout its life. The natural law prescribes that a human acts according to reason and this is what distinguish humans from other creatures. This also gives humans the right to dominate those creatures. Such rights are inalienable and valid beyond the positive law issued by human beings. Following this argumentation, beings that are not rational can have no rights. Apart from the natural law theory, Vitoria also developed the concept of the just war. According to him, war can be unjust if it is waged against the innocent. As long as Indians do not interrupt Spanish expansion, the war against them would be lawless. But simultaneously, Vitoria admitted the war in a situation when foreign nations commit inhuman practices, such as cannibalism or human sacrifice. As he was shaped by the Eurocentric culture, he does not deny the barbarian practices of indigenous groups. However, he never justified the abuses of the Conquest[41].

As we see, all previously mentioned philosophers were of European origin and were shaped by their European heritage hence, the question arises: is it Latin American thought? The answer can be affirmative. Those figures and its writings are strictly related with Latin American affairs of the 16th century. European thought, mainly

---

[41] *Ibidem*, pp. 124-125.

of Spanish philosophers is an almost unique reflection on the issues related to the New World. Of course, it is of a strongly Eurocentric nature. It is also undeniable that it has imperial nature. And there are very few reasons for not describing it as a very early example of colonial imperialism. But there is also no reason for not regarding it as a base that creates a foundation for the development of modern Latin American thought. There are very few examples of Latin American thought in the sense that it is the product of Latin Americans. It immediately creates the question who was Latin American in the colonial period. Representatives of the native population of the New World, creoles, those who lived in America? It is necessary to mention the pre-hispanic texts such as, for example the *Popol Vuh* book. This is a Mayan description of the creation to the historical events of the mid-16th century. The existing copy was made in 1701 by the Dominican clergyman. Another source of the native thought is Bernardino Sahagún's *General History of the Things of New Spain*, commonly known as the *Florence Codex*. It is a text based on the relations of indigenous informants of the Franciscan friar. The result of those native relations is a detailed description of the Aztec religion, daily life, arts, history, philosophy and medical knowledge. In his address to Spanish king Phillip II Felipe Guamán Poma de Ayala, a native Andean philosopher, gave a detailed description of the Andean world, criticizing colonialism and the abuses carried out by European conquistadors. It is worth invoking those examples of indigenous writings as they constitute a part – albeit very small however existing and important – of native Latin American thought. Also, they deny the barbarian image of the New World inhabitants, as they present a high level of cultural and intellectual development of native cultures of America[42].

---

[42] L. F. Restrepo, *Colonial Thought*, [in:] S. Nuccetelli, O. Schutte, O. Bueno, *op. cit.*, p. 44.

Therefore, as Gracia pointed out the problem of AmerIndians, is "[p]erhaps the oldest distinctive philosophical problem of post-Columbian Latin American philosophy concerns the rights of indigenous populations in the Americas, and the duties of those governments that claimed jurisdiction over them"[43].

## PARADIGMS IN LATIN AMERICAN THOUGHT

We intend to use the term paradigms in the classical meaning given by Thomas Kuhn, who coined its contemporary meaning in his book *The Structure of Scientific Revolutions* published in 1962. Kuhn defined a scientific paradigm as: "universally recognized scientific achievements that, for a time, provide model problems and solutions for a community of practitioners"[44]. We identified the list of paradigms that were adopted in research about Latin American thought and are currently used by the researcher. The list we created is provided just for explanatory purposes, we do not perceive it as a definite, we believe that it might be expanded in and built up. In this context, it is essential to keep in mind that the boundaries between various paradigms, that we identified, are hard to clearly outline. Sometimes in their works, thinkers adopt multiple paradigms to prove their point of view. Also, many of those paradigms are in close correlation with each other, therefore adopting one of them might lead to the use of another. We also decided to draw those paradigms in the broadest possible sense, therefore, each of them can

---

[43] J. J. E. Gracia, M. Vargas, *Latin American Philosophy*, [in:] *The Stanford Encyclopedia of Philosophy*, (Fall 2013 Edition), E. N. Zalta (ed.), http://plato.stanford.edu/archives/fall2013/entries/latin-american-philosophy/ (01.09.2015).

[44] Th. S. Kuhn, *The Structure of Scientific Revolutions*, 3rd ed., Chicago, University of Chicago Press, 1996, p. 10.

encompass various research questions and research themes. They are as follows:

1) The question of cultural imperialism
2) The question of existence and identity
3) The question of conquest
4) The question of modernization

When we look at the passage from Robert J. C. Young we will see its interconnectivity of those paradigms[45] – "Colonial and imperial rule was legitimized by anthropological theories which increasingly portrayed the peoples of the colonized world as inferior, childlike, or feminine, incapable of looking after themselves (despite having done so perfectly well for millennia) and requiring the paternal rule of the west for their own best interests (today they are deemed to require 'development'). The basis of such anthropological theories was the concept of race. In simple terms, the west – non-west relation was thought of in terms of whites versus the non-white races"[46].

# THE QUESTION OF CULTURAL IMPERIALISM

The term "cultural imperialism" was coined by Ernest Schiller in 1960s and was applied mainly toward a theory of mass communication. Schiller defined it as "the sum of the process by which a society

---

[45] We decided to exclude post-colonialism from the paradigms, due to various reasons. A majority of them were mentioned in Fernando Coronil: the shockingly poor coverage of Latin America within the fields of postcolonial studies. As Coronil mentioned, this exclusion started with Said's *Culture and Imperialism*. This exclusion was reflected also in the absence of Latin America in the early anthologies dedicated to post-colonialism. Cf. F. Coronil, *Latin American Postcolonial Studies and Global Decolonization*, [in:] N. Lazarus, *The Cambridge Companion to Postcolonial Literary Studies*, Cambridge, Cambridge University Press, 2004, p. 221-240.

[46] R. A. Young, *Postcolonialism*, Oxford, Oxford University Press, 2003, p. 2.

is brought into the modern world system and how its dominating stratum is attracted, pressured, forced and sometimes bribed into shaping social institutions to correspond to or even to promote, the values and structures of the dominant center of the system"[47]. Later on the notion of "cultural imperialism" was filtered through post-structuralism and post-colonialism, mainly by Edward Said and his *Culture and Imperialism.*

As John Tomlison put it "The concept of cultural imperialism does not have a particularly long history. It seems to have emerged, along with many other terms of radical criticism, in the 1960s and has endured becoming part of the general intellectual currency of the second half of the twentieth century. There is no shortage of attempted definitions of the term"[48]. But Tomlison refers to Mattelart to show complexity and contextuality of this notion. "It is always with a certain apprehension that the problem of imperialism is approached and especially what is known as cultural imperialism. This generic concept has too often been used with ill-defined meaning"[49]. But then again, the ill-defined meaning and difficulty with the proper definition are not the only obstacle in the appropriation of this term.

Chris Baker raised quite a serious reservation toward the applicability of this term in the contemporary world. "There are three central difficulties with the cultural imperialism thesis under contemporary conditions. First, it is no longer the case, if it ever was, that the global flows of cultural discourses are constituted as one-way traffic. Second, in so far as the predominant flow of cultural

---

[47]  H. I. S c h i l l e r, *Communication and Cultural Domination*, White Plains, New York, International Arts and Sciences Press, 1976, p. 9.

[48]  J. Tomlinson, *Cultural Imperialism: A Critical Introduction*, Baltimore, Maryland, Johns Hopkins University Press, 1991, pp. 2-3.

[49]  A. Mattelart, S. Siegelaub, *Communication and Class Struggle: An Anthology in 2 Volumes*, Vol. 1, New York, International General, 1979, p. 57.

discourse remains from West to East and North to South, this is not *necessarily* a form of domination. Third, it is unclear that the current period of globalization represents a simple process of homogenization since the forces of fragmentation and hybridity are equally as strong"[50].

However we can agree that the global flows of cultural discourses are constituted as one-way traffic, but it still lacks the true reciprocity. So far, we introduced a lot of examples showing the difficulties in the research of Latin American thought caused by the obstacle in the lack of adequate materials. The question should be raised why we still can observe such a shocking lack of adequate materials and to what extent it is caused by the common perception made from the position of the cultural "center" recognizing non-center intellectual activities as peripheral and not worth the investigation.

We cannot support the claim that "the predominant flow of cultural discourse remains from West to East and North to South, this is not *necessarily* a form of domination". The fact that the direction of the predominant flow of the cultural discourse is parallel with what has been perceived through centuries as the valuable and superior culture, thought and philosophy is a form of domination, and the imposition of such a system of cultural values that originated in the North/West and are more worthy of investigation than those that were created on the South/East.

Therefore, the moment of recognition and awareness of the existence of such a cultural imperialist attitude in the perception of Latin American thought is extremely important. It is essential to keep in mind that such recognition was made by the both sides: those that were part of the North/West discourse and those who were part of the South/East discourse. The first group was able to adopt a more

---

[50] Ch. Barker, *The Sage Dictionary of Cultural Studies*, London, Sage Publications, 2004, p. 38.

inclusive approach toward the non-Western systems of thought and philosophy. This is also visible in the gradual development of area studies, deeply rooted in cultural localities. The other group realized that some element of intellectual discourse subconsciously caused labeling and out ruling of the presence of non-Western philosophical systems as the equal contribution toward the global discourse. This was paired with the consciousness about the "hybridity" of Latin American thought which was so strongly rooted in the locality, and at the same time aspires to reach the western philosophical core and find global recognition. Such an understanding was also crucial for the appearance of another paradigm – conceptual decolonization which has been correlated with intellectual liberalization and emancipation from the Western/Northern imposition.

As it can be observed, the early period of creating Latin American thought is restricted to two areas. The first one, namely the principal aim of Latin American thought realized by Europeans, is dedicated to the question of Indian's humanity and to the justification of the European conquest of the New World. It imposes the European perspective and European values on the judgment as to what is worth exploring and what discourses should be silenced out. This is well exemplified by Sepúlveda, las Casas, Vitoria, and others. The second one, the product of both Europeans and very few native Americans, is of a descriptive nature. Europeans were getting to know the new continent. They explored and described it. Meanwhile, the above-mentioned native writings are of the nature of a historical description of the world of its inhabitants.

This situation has changed with the passing of time. Latin American thought was still determined by European doctrines, especially scholasticism, but it also changed slightly. First, it was less descriptive and more analyzing. Second, it was more Latin American, in the sense that at that moment it was to the higher degree a product of Latin Americans. It is important to remember that Latin American thought in its modern form – since the encounter of the Old World and the New one – was created under the great influence of European philosophy. It is the effect of total domination of the New World by Europeans, more specifically, Spaniards and Portugueses. They dominated the new continent militarily, politically, economically, socially, and culturally. Political and economic colonialism existed from the beginning of the 16th century until the first years of the 19th century, as did cultural imperialism. It had a great impact on the development of philosophy and thought in Latin America. In fact, most of the Latin American philosophers in the colonial period, but also later, had European roots. There cannot be any doubt that such figures as Garcilaso de la Vega known as "El Inca", Alva Ixtlixóchitl or Sor Juana were Latin American creators of Latin American thought. The first one was the son of an Inca princess and a Spanish captain. As a child he grew up in the Inca tradition, however as a young man, he was under his father's protection and was brought up in Spanish tradition. As a mature man, he lived in Spain. Though, in his writings – with famous *Comentarios reales* – he insisted on his Indian roots[51].

This shows the existing dichotomy between the adoption of European canons and frames on the one hand, and the quest for independent, distinct, and more "Latin American" flavored elements. This dichotomy was expressed in the quest for proper methods and paradigms. Some thinkers followed the European methodological path, adopting the European patterns for the quest, investigation, and validation of knowledge. While others tried to adopt either the European school of thought and European methodological approaches to the Latin American reality or develop new paradigms that would be uniquely applicable to the Latin American intellectual reality.

---

[51] Polish edition: I. G. de la Vega, *O Inkach uwagi prawdziwe*, Warsaw, CESLA, 2000 (*Comentarios reales de los Incas*).

# THE QUESTION OF IDENTITY

It is hard to overestimate the importance of the question of identity; it is one of the leading notions, being of a complex nature and creating far-reaching consequences. As Gracia stated: "The question of identity and Latin American philosophy has been a topic of intense discussion among Latin Americans. It has two major parts. The first concerns the identity *of* Latin American philosophy itself; the second concerns how identity has been discussed *in* Latin American philosophy. The first may, in turn, be divided into at least two sub-topics: whether in fact there is such a thing as Latin American philosophy and how best to conceive it. The division of the second depends on the identity of which things have been discussed by Latin American philosophers. The most important among these is the identity of the Latin American peoples, and especially of ethnic, racial, and national identities"[52].

This search started in the mid-1920s and in 1930s, and according to Rabossi "[b]y 1925-30, a most interesting controversy began to unfold. (…) The controversy was about the identity and aims of Latin American philosophising. A large number of issues were involved: the unrestricted universality attributed to philosophical statements, problems, and theories versus a restricted, 'located', universality or, even, sheer particularism; the cosmopolitan airs of philosophy versus a regional or national élan; the possibility of an original and authentic philosophical thinking versus a dependent, importative, or imitative one; the seemingly economic, political, and ideological neutrality of philosophy versus the assumption of its real, earthly, commitments; the impact of philosophy in everyday affairs versus its abstract and detached condition. The controversy turned on the description and evaluation of the practice of philosophy in

---

[52]  J. J. E. Gracia, *Identity and Latin American....*

Latin America: how to *assess* the value of the professional practice of philosophy; what sort of *diagnosis* its shortcomings, deficiencies, and frailties merited; what a proper *prognosis* of its course of development would be; what philosophy *ought* to do and achieve in Latin America. These different topics, obviously related, were very often mixed up"[53].

Some of the Latin American thinkers refer to the so-called philosophy of liberation as the most explicit manifestation of Latin American thought autonomy. It is an attempt to confirm cultural and intellectual sovereignty of the region. The philosophy of liberation proclaims that Latin American thought is Latin American not because it concerns on the region but because it grows up from the Latin American context and its culture[54]. Pablo Neruda, Manuel González Prada, José María Arteguas are the most prominent representatives of this current of Latin American thought. Enrique Dussel also refers to the philosophy of liberation and explains that this is a kind of response to cultural imperialism, of which Latin America is a victim. "An 'imperial' culture (that of the core), which originated with the invasion of America in 1492, confronted with the 'peripheral' cultures in Latin America, Africa, Asia and Eastern Europe. The result was not a symmetrical dialogue, but rather one of domination, of exploitation, of annihilation. Moreover, the elites of these 'peripheral cultures' were educated by the imperialist"[55].

The arguments used by the representatives of this current are quite different from notions presented by Leopoldo Zea but the conclusion is common. Latin American thought, philosophy and culture exists. The impact of European or occidental ideas is unquestionable.

---

[53] E. Rabossi, *Latin American…*, p. 511.

[54] R. Fornet-Betancourt, *La filosofía de liberación en América Latina*, [in:] G. E. Forment, *Filosofía de hispanoamérica. Aproximaciones al panorama actual*, Barcelona, ICE, University of Barcelona, 1987, p. 125.

[55] E. Dussel, *op. cit.*, pp. 6-7.

This influence is perceived in different ways, as something natural (Leopoldo Zea) or as the effect of cultural imperialism (philosophy of liberation) but it does not signify that the region does not create its own intellectual reflection. A great debate related to the identity of Latin America and Latin Americans that takes place nowadays confirms that thesis. Latin Americans are conscious of their distinction, however, they are also conscious of the fact that they belong to the occidental culture which has a great impact on their cultural and intellectual development.

# THE QUESTION OF CONQUEST

As Walter D. Mignolo pointed out "Americas exist today only as a consequence of European colonial expansion and the narrative of that expansion from the European perspective, the perspective of modernity (…). To illustrate [this], consider that a Christian and Marxist analysis of a given event, say the 'discovery of America' would offer us different interpretations; that *both would be from the perspective of modernity*. That is, the 'discovery of America' would be seen in both cases *from the perspective of Europe*"[56]. Also, Leopoldo Zea pointed out the importance of knowledge about the past and the need for deep awareness. "[O]ne of the most painful things to remember and assume as part of one's Latin American heritage is the event of the conquest. Why is this so? On the one hand, there were Aztecs in Mexico, mistaking the Spanish conquerors for gods, and therefore, committing cultural suicide"[57].

The conquest itself has far-reaching consequences: "the phenomenon of imperial expansion has, in the Western world, a genealogy

---

[56] W. Mignolo, *The Idea of Latin America*, Malden, Maryland, Blackwell Pub., 2005, p. XI.
[57] O. Schutte, *op. cit.*, p. 112.

that is much longer and more complex than the one generally considered by postcolonial studies. Spanish and Portuguese colonialism triggered, during the sixteenth and seventeenth centuries, a long series of political, economic, and cultural processes which-with the support of an intricate and diversified web of projects and discourses-instituted modernity as the space of intelligibility where colonial domination could be implemented and legitimized as the strategy that would allow the installation and consolidation of Western civilization as defined by metropolitan standards. With the emergence of Spanish colonialism at the end of the fifteenth century and not just with the Enlightenment, as is usually assumed by postcolonial studies-Eurocentrism became a conceptual and a political reality, and the periphery emerged as the repository of material and symbolic commodities that would nurture, from then on, the economies and cultures of the Old World"[58].

## THE QUESTION OF MODERNIZATION

The strive toward modernization seems to be another constitutive element in Latin America thought. Hurtado attempts to trace the long history of this quest toward modernization. "The phenomenon of modernization in our philosophy goes back to the eighteenth century when a movement of opening toward modern science and modern philosophy took place in Spain, Portugal, and their colonies in the American continent. It was in the third quarter of the nineteenth century, with the arrival of positivism, that a series of what we might call "modernizing movements" began in our

---

[58] M. Moraña, E. D. Dussel, C. A. Jáuregui, *Coloniality at Large: Latin America and the Postcolonial Debate*, Durham, Duke University Press, 2008, p. 8.

philosophy. Although there are important differences in each country, we may say that since then we have had at least four modernizing movements:

1. Positivist modernization arose during the second half of the 19th century. Latin American positivism presented itself as the philosophy required for the social and material progress of our people. (…)

2. After the downfall of positivism, a large modernization of German origin began, disseminating various lines of thought such as neo-Kantism, historicism, axiology, phenomenology, and existentialism. The influence of Ortega and *Revista de Occidente* had much to do with this phenomenon. This is also the period when the pupils of the founding masters worked toward what Francisco Romero called the *normalization* of Latin American philosophy. (…)

3. In the first half of the twentieth century a Marxist modernization also began, the influences and orientations of which were very diverse: from Marx and Gramsci to Bloch and Althusser. This movement – which like the positivist one intended to influence social reality – addressed a wide spectrum of philosophical problems ranging from logic to aesthetics. (…)

4. Finally, analytic modernization began toward the end of the 1950s, (…) stand out among the founding figures of this movement. The analytic philosophers provided another impulse to the task of the normalization of Latin American philosophy; they put an emphasis on the mastery of techniques, such as formal logic; on knowledge of the sciences, like the positivists did before them; and on the rigor of philosophical work"[59].

This drive toward *modernidad* might partially explain the extraordinary popularity of positivism in Latin America. A radical rejection of the Scholastic paradigm in intellectual considerations and

---

[59] G. Hurtado, *Two Models…*, pp. 204-205.

new tendencies and paradigms appeared in Latin American thought at the beginning of the 19th century. It coincided with the collapse of the European colonial empires in Latin America. The wars for independence not only brought political sovereignty from old metropolis but were also an important step toward Latin American thought more independent from European influence. The most important was a final rejection of the dominance of the Scholastic paradigm. Latin American intellectuals were aware of the existence of new philosophical doctrines and tendencies that were already gaining dominance in European philosophy since the 18th century. These new theories, unlike the scholastic ones, were based on rationalism and empirism. In this situation, colonial emancipation was accompanied by the new intellectual awakening. As there were political and military liberators, there were also intellectual precursors of new trends in Latin American thought. The one that was still inspired by European philosophical fundaments but now with more specific accents that have made it more Latin American. The main subjects of Latin American thought in the first part of the 19th century were closely related to the situation in the region. The successful wars for independence, throwing off the colonial chains and the formation of new, independent states produced new problems, new situations and new challenges for Latin American intellectuals. In effect, the difference between Latin American thought during the colonial period and after the independence is quite explicit. The colonial discourse was dominated by the metaphysical considerations over the question of indigenous people and their place in the colonial society, the just or unjust nature of the conquest, the nature of the human being, meanwhile, the first decades of independence were dominated by questions about the nature and character of political systems, especially the new incarnation of democracy presented by the former British colonies in North America. The political emancipation was accompanied by the necessity of mental emancipation. However, the appearance of those new aspects of Latin American thought do not meant a complete resignation from the previous areas of interest[60].

It it worth mentioning the great liberator and the father of Latin American independence, Simón Bolívar as the first representative of those new tendencies in Latin American thought. As he was Creole, he was naturally under the influence of European culture. It did not prevent him from perceiving Latin American specificity and distinction. He wrote: "We are not Europeans; we are not Indians, we are but the mixed species of aborigines and Spaniards. Americans by birth and Europeans by law, we find ourselves engaged in a dual conflict: we are disputing with natives for titles of ownership, and at the same time we are struggling to maintain ourselves in the country that gave birth against the opposition of the invaders"[61].

As he was a practitioner of the new Latin American reality in the first decades of the 19th century, it is obvious that most of his considerations were related to the form of newly emerged sovereign states. But also, in this area, he saw distinct characteristics of the region – both geographic and physical but also social and cultural. Those distinctions produced significant repercussions. The main conclusion was, that as Latin America and Europe, in fact, are so various, they therefore also require different forms of government. "Laws must take into account the physical conditions of the country, climate, character of the land, location, size, and mode of living of the people"[62]. This awareness resulted in Bolivar's admiration of the political system of the United States, he was convinced that it is impossible to introduce it in the new states of Latin America. Equally, he was completely convinced that the monarchical systems

---

[60] C. Candia Baeza, *Filosofia, identidad y pensamiento político en Latinoamérica*, "Polis: Revista Académica de la Universidad Bolivariana" 2008, No. 18.

[61] S. Bolivar, *Message to the Congress of Angostura, 1819*, http://www.fordham.edu/HALSAll/MOD/1819bolivar.asp (27.09.2012).

[62] *Ibidem.*

of Europe do not suit Latin American conditions. That is why, he was desperately devoted to the promotion of the republican system, but he simultaneously understood the necessity of a strong, central authority. As he said, "[Latin – K. D.] America is ungovernable". That explains why it needed strong authority. A brief look on the history of Latin American states proves that this observation was quite accurate and Latin American states had great problems with forming stable governments.

The emergence of new, independent states in the Latin American region formed conditions for intellectual awakening. Latin Americans, liberated from European or Iberian dominance had to look for their own solutions of their problems. Even though this intellectual awakening was based on the foundation created in Europe (which is quite natural since in Europe, especially in France and England the most influential intellectual doctrines and theories originated at that time). But those, in the 19th century, were successfully transformed by Latin American intellectuals and have been adapted to the unique situation of the region. That is why the Latin American thought in the 19th century was developed and enriched. This period resulted in the further "latinamericanization" of Latin American thought. This new tendency also marked the beginning of positivism in Latin America. This period in the development of Latin American thought brought vast numbers of prominent Latin American philosophers and intellectuals. It also opened Latin American thought to new areas that until the second half of the 19th century were not the subject of deep reflection in the region. Undoubtedly, Latin American positivism was a response for the problems that harassed the new states. There was a great effort in changing old habits and customs formulated during the colonial period. There was a great necessity of intellectual effort that would respond to the need of self-awareness and progress.

Representatives of Latin American positivist intelligentsia understood pretty well that the simple adoption of European thought is not enough. Moreover, the simple adoption of positivist ideas in Latin America would not be proper. It is essential to keep in mind that in those times Latin American societies were much more complicated than European ones. There were not only class divisions but also racial, ethnic, social, cultural etc. ones. That is why some aspects of European positivist thought were accented more strongly in Latin America than in Europe. For example, the racial problem, the case of political stability, economic development or education was probably more important for Latin Americans than for a majority of citizens in European countries. Also, solutions that have been proposed by Latin American positivists sometimes varied from those proposed by Europeans and they did not restrain themselves from free interpretations of European ideas[63]. Latin American positivism, as an exemplification of Latin American thought in the second half of the 19th century expressed itself most clearly in the appeal for progress and reform through education. As it is easy to observe, those elements are new ones in Latin American thought. It is possible to formulate the conclusion that positivism was dedicated to modernity, which became a fundamental aspect of Latin American thought in the positivist issue. This was the result of Latin American intellectuals' who studied "progress" and the evolution of knowledge, society, and the law in order to reform them. Elites wanted to establish national sovereignty, and defend "civilization". In the early years of independence, Latin American elites tried different solutions to find the best way of progress and development in every sphere of public life. First, they wanted governments truly autonomous from their former metropolises. Simultaneously, however, they had no experience and big anxieties because of the ultra-complicated nature of postcolonial societies. They were diverse in nearly every possible

---

[63]  G. Horváth, S. Szabó, *El positivismo en Brasil y México. Un estudio comparativo*, "Tzintzun. Revista de Estudios Históricos" 2005, No. 42, p. 10.

dimension. Multiracial, multicultural, with deep social, political and economic divisions[64]. That is why, as never before, Latin American elites recognized the need to create their own solutions for problems particular to the region. As progress was the main goal, every action should be aimed for the implementation of new solutions that would help to reach this end. That explains, for example, the big popularity of thesis that only a Latin America based on European patterns can reach progress. Juan Bautista Alberdi said that European presence in Latin America is nothing new. Moreover, that presence could be perceived as a real blessing and independent Latin America is a product of Europe. "South American Republics are the fruit and the live testimony of European activity in America. Independent America is nothing more than Europe established in America; our revolution is nothing more than the division of European power into parts that are now self-governing"[65]. By reaching the New World, every European, as Alberdi believed, enriched Latin American civilization. There was no place for indigenous communities in the idea of Latin America created on European resemblance. The only proposition for them was the adoption of European cultural patterns. Similar reflections were presented by the other Argentinean representatives of positivism, Domingo Faustino Sarmiento. According to him, the best remedy for the problems of Latin American republics is European immigration.

---

[64] M. L. Clark, *The Emergence and Transformation of Positivism*, [in:] S. Nuccetelli, O. Schutte, O. Bueno, *A Companion to Latin...*, p. 55.

[65] "Las Repúblicas de la America se Sur son producto y testimonio vivo de la acción de Europa en America. Lo que llamamos America independiente no es mas que Europa establecida en America; nuestra revolución no es otra cosa que la desmembración de un poder europeo en dos mitades, que hoy se manejan por sí mismas", J. B. Alberdi, *Bases y puntos de partida para la organización política de la Republica Argentina*, [in:] L. Zea, *Pensamiento positivista latinoamericano*, Caracas, Venezuela, Biblioteca Ayacucho, 1980, p. 79.

At the level of intellectual and philosophical dispute, Latin American positivism was originally cultivated to encourage the growth of science, and in the hands of liberals like Gabino Barreda, as a weapon for breaking the intellectual stranglehold of conservative mentality and for refuting the claims of scholasticism. If positivism had proven to be an intellectually useful tool against scholasticism, some Latin Americans saw, at least, some of its assumptions as unsatisfactory and many of its implications as unacceptable[66]. An important change of accent in Latin American thought could also be observed at the turn of the 19th and 20th century. One of the most important topics of Latin American thought appeared to be the question about the identity, partially as a product of anti-positivist criticism. José Enrique Rodó's *Ariel* is a fundamental writing for the issue of identity. Underlying the youth of Latin American nations, he points to their common heritage rooted in ancient Greece and Rome. Rodó presents a very harsh critique of the United States. For him, North America is the paradigm of barbarism. In this way, he opposed Latin America – based on the Mediterranean civilization derived on the Greek and Christian Roman culture – to North America. Carlos Fuentes, a great Mexican intellectual, gave a good summary of Rodó's considerations related to Latin American identity. He wrote that "...Rodó's Ariel appear as the emotional and intellectual response of Latin American thought and Latin American spirituality to growing North American imperial arrogance, gunboat diplomacy, and big stick policies"[67]. Though, it is hard to omit a significant controversy connected to Rodó's conception – it is radically Eurocentric. It is true that Latin American culture is based to a significant degree on European roots. However, it is inadmissible to ig-

---

[66] O. R. Martí, *Early Critics of Positivism*, [in:] S. Nuccetelli, O. Schutte, O. Bueno, *op. cit.*, pp. 69-70.

[67] C. Fuentes, *Prolog to José Enrique Rodó: Ariel*, Austin, University of Texas Press, 1988, p. 16.

nore the entire Latin American peculiarity resultant from its cultural diversity and ethnic heterogeneity. This individual nature of Latin America was already mentioned by Simón Bolívar and underlined in the end of the 19th century by Cuban intellectual José Martí. In his most popular writing, *Nuestra América*, he contested the racism of Spencerians as Sarmiento because they accepted only immediate material conditions as evidence yet ignored historical and cultural factors. Backwardness in Latin America was the result of political and economic exploitation by colonial powers and of the effort of industrial nations to keep it economically dependent. Evolutionary theory, if anything, is a rationalization of rich countries for allotting a lesser treatment of the poorer ones[68]. Also, he took up the topic of economic and social development. Sometimes he is described as a precursor of social justice in Latin America. His reflections about the exploitation of the individual and postcolonial nations prepared the ground for the later expansion of Marxist and socialist ideology in the region.

## METHODS TYPICAL FOR OTHER AREAS – POLITICAL, SOCIAL AND CULTURAL THOUGHT, APPLICABLE TO THE QUEST FOR LATIN AMERICAN THOUGHT

Ofelia Schutte wrote that "Latin American philosophy tends to be highly self-conscious about the question of methodology. The adoption of the particular methodology can usually be linked to the impact of major schools of European and Anglo-American on the continent. For example, the influence of positivism during the latter part of the nineteenth century and the reactions he gains this philosophical school in the early part of the twentieth century have played a large role in the development of Latin American thought.

---

[68]  O. R. Martí, *Early Critics...*, p. 71.

The importance given to methodology such, however, may be much older – it is very possibly a carryover from the scholastic tradition transplanted into the region during colonial times"[69].

Then she mentioned more universally recognized schools of thought that "rest on accepted and well-defined methodologies". They include: philosophical Marxism, post-Hegelian historicism, Christian perspective on liberation, Anglo-American analytic philosophy, and the feminist approach. But Schutte is aware of the difficulties to describe thinkers to the aforementioned schools of thought. "Not all writers (…) share pluralistic theoretical perspective just articulated. It will be seen that, more often than not, grand theories have been constructed to account for an 'authentic' interpretation of history or a 'correct' version of regional cultural identity"[70].

As we might observe, in terms of methodology, Latin American thought, on the one hand, shares a methodological approach with the Western world, on the other hand, is preoccupied with "authentic' interpretation of history or a 'correct' version of regional cultural identity". However, we are more willing to associate this quest for historical authenticity and correctness of cultural identity with the scientific investigation we described and identified exit paradigms such as Latin American thought.

## DISCOURSE ANALYSIS OR LINGUISTIC APPROACH

"Discourse analysis (DA) is best seen as a cluster of related methods for studying language use and its role in social life. Some of these methods study language use with a particular interest in its coherence over sentences or turns, its role in constructing the world, and

---

[69] O. Schutte, *op. cit.*, p. 2.
[70] *Ibidem*, p. 3.

its relationship to context. Others take discourses to be objects in their own right that can be described and counted. This entry identifies a range of terminological confusions, discusses some of the origins of DA, and describes the main contemporary approaches"[71]. It is based on proper historical understanding of the activity of thinking becomes possible only if we view it in terms of statements made at a particular date by a particular person in a certain context. In research on Latin American thought it appears to be the most common methodological approach among scholars.

## FEMINIST APPROACH

The feminist critique has exposed the misogynist assumptions underlying the thought of great male political theorists from Plato to Marx. It is based on the assumption that "Feminist epistemology brings together the usual epistemological concerns such as what constitutes knowledge and how it is constructed with the central issues of feminist theory: gender as an analytic category. (…) [A]t their roots is the consideration of the role of gender in determining how knowledge is constructed, both by individual knowers and by social and cultural groups of women and men. A theme in many discussions is how power relations based on gender (and race, culture, social class, and other social categories) shape what counts as knowledge in debates not only in epistemology and feminist theory, but also in all academic disciplines. Given that the purpose of all research is ultimately to produce knowledge and since feminist epistemology brings out the role of gender in shaping knowledge construction, gender is important in considerations of all research

---

[71] J. Potter, *Discourse Analysis*, [in:] L. M. Given, *The Sage Encyclopedia of Qualitative Research Methods*, Los Angeles, Calif., Sage Publications, 2008, p. 218.

methodology. It is especially relevant in discussions of qualitative research where the researcher is very consciously involved in and part of the research process. This entry first gives an overview of feminist theories and then describes differences and similarities between theories that focus on the individual, structural, cultural, and standpoint feminist theories; and post-structural, post-modern, and post-colonial feminist theories. Lastly, it discusses the ways in which these feminist perspectives affect the conduct and analysis of research"[72].

The earliest example of feminist epistemology can be associated with the iconic Juana Inés de la Cruz, known as Sor (Sister) Juana. She is exceptional example of philosophers of those times. First of all, she was a woman. Her writings are a good illustration of limitations of colonial society in the New World and its scholastic paradigm. Also, she was a precursor of the discussion related to the rights of women. Sometimes she is called the first feminist as she explained women's right to education and knowledge. However, she cannot be described as a feminist in the contemporary meaning of this word, she rather insisted that women are rational beings so they should be guaranteed the same rights as men, also in the area of education. As Susana Nuccetelli writes, there is no doubt that Juana Ines' attitude toward knowledge and women's rights must have been perceived as a menace by practitioners of the scholastic paradigm, who dominated the intellectual life of New Spain. She seems to have held that beliefs about the world must be grounded in the natural sciences and in one's own empirical experience[73]. Similarly, it is no doubt that in the scholastic reality of New Spain, Sor Juana's writings and conclusions were developing a modern thought. They

---

[72] E. J. Tisdell, *Feminist Epistemology*, [in:] L. M. Given, *op. cit.*, p. 331.
[73] S. Nuccetelli, O. Schutte, O. Bueno, *op. cit.*, pp. 156-157.

consisted a modern revolution to rid New Spain of the old scholastic paradigm.

## THE MARXIST APPROACH

The Marxist approach is built mainly on the tendency to examine ideas in terms of ideologies rooted in a particular mode of production In Latin America, the critique of the United States and its capitalist economic system that appeared in the end of the 19th century, gained a great popularity in the following decades. It is Peruvian thinker, José Carlos Mariátegui, who is perceived as one of the precursors of socialist ideas in Latin America. He continued José Martí's skepticism about and rejection of US-styled socio-economic development. According to him, Latin American cultural and social specificity makes it impossible to introduce the North American pattern. His most important accusation was that the capitalist system treats social justice like dirt. Mariátegui shared the conviction that justice was not possible within capitalism with other Marxist and socialists of his time. In his opinion, capitalism always produces social and economic inequalities because some own the means of production and others only the ability to work, which they must then sell in a free market at whatever price the owners of those means find appropriate to pay. Mariátegui's views on social – economic development enriched Latin American thought about this aspect. After years of liberal dominance in the sphere of the Latin American economy in the second half of the 19th century, the beginning of the 20th century was marked by the growing popularity of more or less radical socialist ideas.

Mariátegui was also the precursor – or one of the very first thinkers since Bartolomé de las Casas – to be a strong defender of the indigenous population in the region. He was Peruvian so he knew the situation of Indians very precisely as Peru had one of the biggest indigenous populations. In his opinion, Indians were suffering permanent injustice and persecutions. This situation had been taking place since the Conquest. He called it the "Indian question" and explained that all those inequities were the effect of the "imported" feudal system and unfair distribution of the land imposed by the colonial empires[74]. He was a strong opponent of positivist view expressed in a most radical way by Sarmiento that all that is Latin American means barbarism. Mariátegui underlined that Indians do not represent barbarism. According to him, they had the same abilities to assimilate progressive techniques of modern production as the mestizo people.

Mariátegui's considerations, however, grounded strongly in Latin American reality, where also inspired by European thought. These do not deny the originality of Latin American thought. Rodó, Martí, Mariátegui are only a few examples of the development of Latin American thought in the end of the 19th century and in the first decades of the 20th century. The thought was still developing. Earlier elements were constantly added to new ones, as reflections on social development, economic independence, anti-imperialism have been understood not only as a rejection of the old colonial metropolis, but also as opposition to the emergence of new power in the form of the United States of America, much closer to the Latin America than European declining superpowers. All those elements grounded deeply in Latin American realities resulted in the development of specific and original Latin American thought. One more element that to this days constitutes an ultra important part of Latin American thought also appeared and continued to develop. Undoubtedly, it was the consequence of both the changing realities of the region and growing self-awareness of its inhabitants. One of the most important factors that increased the necessity to explain the identity

---

[74] S. Nuccetelli, *op. cit.*, pp. 204-207.

of Latin Americans was the growing expansionism of the United States. The consciousness of the multiplicity of Latin America played an important role in the formulation of its identity. To the question *"Who are we?"* famous Mexican thinker José Vasconselos provided answer in his *"Cosmic Race"*. By this description he meant a specific race that emerged from the marriage of Indians, Europeans, Africans, Americans, Asians, Africans – mestizo. This unique marriage resulted in the formation of the new race, the Cosmic Race, that comprises the best characteristics of the human and is its best expression. Meanwhile, Argentinean philosopher Enrique Dussel asked: "Who we are culturally? What is our historical identity?" In his answer to these questions, he explained that Latin America had his place within the process of human development since the origins of the homo species, Before Christ, and up to the encounter of the Old and New World in 1492[75]. As we analyze paradigms in Latin American thought, the questions of identity and self-awareness had never been so important as in the 20th century. Thus, it should not be surprising that the most important Latin American thinkers and philosophers raised this question. It was Bolivar and later Martí, Mariátegui or Vasconselos who first undertook the question of Latin American identity, but it is the second half of 20th century when the subject emerged as one of the central points of Latin American thought. Another great Mexican philosopher, Leopoldo Zea, was deeply engaged in the debate about the identity of the region. According to him, the most important characteristic of Latin American philosophy is an ability to assimilate components imported from outside of the region to its very peculiar realities and necessities. He argued that the real problem is not the pursuit of the discovery

---

[75] E. Dussel, *Transmodernity and Interculturality: An Interpretation from the Perspective of Philosophy of Liberation*, "Transmodernity: Journal of Peripheral Cultural Production of the Luso-Hispanic World" 2012, Vol. 3, No. 1, pp. 1-2.

of hidden truths but the ability to respond to real requirements that are changing. He strongly advocates the existence of Latin American thought and philosophy which is proven by the continuity and perpetual endeavor to explain Latin American reality and problems. Functioning in the environment of occidental culture, Latin America was able and still is able to elaborate its own particular identity[76].


## POSTMODERNISM

Postmodernism last but not least is "[p]erhaps the most radically transformative intellectual movement (or perhaps, more accurately, movements) of the latter part of the 20th century, postmodernism nonetheless defies ready definition. The term, used by Daniel Bell, Jean Francois Lyotard, Mark Poster, and others to describe contemporary, mediasaturated late-capitalist society is also widely, even indiscriminately, used to describe the work of a range of influential Continental philosophers and social thinkers, such as Michel Foucault, Jacques Derrida, and Jean Baudrillard. Postmodernism in the social sciences is strongly associated with a range of approaches to social research, including discourse analysis, post-structuralism, social constructivism, critical theory, feminist and queer theories, and so on. Indeed, ideas associated with postmodernism have become so all-pervasive in contemporary academic discourses, and its proponents and critics have become so numerous, that its influence can be seen in virtually all areas not only of the social sciences from anthropology and sociology to information behavior research and knowledge management but also of the academy as a whole"[77]. Any language unit can be defined only in relation to other units in the

---

[76] C. Candia Baeza, *op. cit.*
[77] M. Olsson, *Postmodernism*, [in:] L. Given (ed.), *op. cit.*, pp. 656-660.

system. A word acquires meaning primarily from the differences between it and other words. Therefore, words do not 'mean' their objects in a transparent manner. It can generate meaning only through the interplay of differences.

Young points out that it's very hard to talk about postmodernism in the Latin American context because it is a "global phenomena which originates outside the continent in the side that does not sure many of the same characteristics, especially in the socio-economy, scientific, and political domain. Indeed it is this global dimension that produces a strong attitude of rejection in Latin America, although they are other reasons for it"[78].

"By creating the possibility of a critical re-reading of modernity, postmodernism offers us the chance to reconsider all that was 'left unsaid' and to inject its areas of opacity and resistance with the potential for new, as yet undiscovered, meanings. In the Latin American context, this review of modernity allows us, once again, to pose the question of our own identity, that of individuals born of and into the dialectic mixture of the different languages surrounding us, which have partially fused to produce a cultural identity experienced as a series of collisions"[79].

"Scientific discourses from this perspective are, therefore, seen not as the privileged discoverers of objective facts, but the product of power-knowledge relations within and between scientific communities and their sociopolitical context. Discourses are sites for generating social agreement but also resistances – changing circumstances and the dynamics of discursive interaction must inevitably give rise to new discourses and new ways of looking at the world. (…) Deconstructionism has been influential in a number of areas of the social sciences, such as sociology and anthropology, where it has been used to

---

[78] R. A. Young, *Latin American Postmodernisms*, Amsterdam, Rodopi, 1997, p. 33.
[79] N. Richard, *Postmodernism and Periphery*, "Third Text" 1987/1988, No. 2, pp. 5-12.

question the authoritative status of traditional ethnographic texts and techniques. The technique has also been used by feminist researchers, for example, to analyze patriarchal discourses"[80].

---

[80] M. R. Olsson, *Postmodernism*, [in:] L. M. Given, *The Sage Encyclopedia of Qualitative Research Methods*, Los Angeles, Calif., Sage Publications, 2008, pp. 656-660.

DOI: 10.12797/9788376386775.03

# II. LATIN AMERICAN POSITIVISM OR POSITIVISM IN LATIN AMERICA?

The most fundamental question we posed in this title can be re-phrased as such: whether one can just talk about the mere imple-mentation of European philosophical currents and ideas in the New World? Or maybe the New World was so disparate, that the Eu-ropean concepts and categories needed to be transformed, adapted and accustomed, in order to be applicable to this new social, intel-lectual and environmental conditions on the Latin American conti-nent. The case of positivism, the philosophical movement so widely disseminated in Latin America and the Caribbean, is the perfect example to illustrate this long lasting debate. Should we talk about positivism as the movement just transplanted into Latin American cultural reality? Or has this movement been transformed so deeply that it achieved a completely new quality, different from its Euro-pean inspiration? Can we call it "Latin American positivism"?

It is not surprising that the Latin American thinkers advocated the culturalists' claims. Latin American intellectuals were persua-sively articulating the existence of distinct Latin American thought. After the period of struggle for independence, those demands for the recognition of Latin American intellectual separateness from the Metropolis were more eagerly expressed. One of the earliest and the most significant of those articulations was the text of Argentinean philosopher Juan Bautista Alberdi. In his speech delivered in 1842 in

Montevideo, *Ideas para presidir a la confección del curso de filosofía contemporánea*, he denied any attempt to transplant European ideas in an unchanged manner. He also questioned the concept of any "universal" philosophy. According to his opinion, philosophy is created as a response to a particular, national needs. Alberdi observed: "Thus there is no universal philosophy, because there is no universal solution to the issues that are at the foundation. Every country, every age, every philosopher has had its unique philosophy, which has spread more or less, which lasted more or less, because every country, every age and every school have different solutions to the problems of the human spirit"[81].

This culturalists approach was applied to the perception of positivism. The hypothesis of the distinctiveness of Latin American positivism was claimed more than a half century ago by Arturo Ardao: "In Latin America, positivism was not only *adopted* but *adapted*. It was adopted, but it had to adapt itself to our historical-cultural characteristics. Its assimilation, therefore, evolved through its transformation"[82]. Ardao also noticed the difference between the "national" version of positivism, observing that the Mexican positivism was different from the Argentinean one. This complexity and incoherence of Latin American positivism was also observed by Meri L. Clark, who believes that Latin American positivism "has

---

[81] "No hay, pues, una filosofía universal, porque no hay una solución universal de las cuestiones que la constituyen en el fondo. Cada país, cada época, cada filósofo ha tenido su filosofía peculiar, que ha cundido más o menos, que ha durado más o menos, porque cada país, cada época y cada escuela han dado soluciones distintas de los problemas del espíritu humano", J. B. Alberdi, *Ideas para presidir a la confección del curso de filosofía contemporánea*, [in:] J. Gaos, *El pensamiento hispanoamericano. Antología del pensamiento de lengua española en la edad contemporánea*, Mexico City, National Autonomous University of Mexico, Coordinación de Humanidades, 1993, p. 332.

[82] A. Ardao, *Assimilation and Transformation of Positivism in Latin America*, "Journal of the History of Ideas" X-XII 1963, Vol. 24, No. 4, p. 515.

been poorly defined, in part, because of the eclectic nature of the thinkers who aligned themselves with the philosophy or who were posthumously aligned with it"[83]. This eclectic nature of positivism in Latin America makes more difficult the attempts to present it as the solid, coherent movement, and to prove that it is so deeply different from its European inspiration.

Nevertheless, we intend to answer the question posed in the title. We will briefly sketch the portrait of European positivism, identifying the most fundamental elements constituting it. Then, examining positivism in Latin America, we can trace those elements that are common with the European core, as well as we can see which elements were neglected, transformed, adapted or hyperbolized to become more appealing to Latin American intellectuals. In identifying those elements that are vital for positivism in Latin America, we will finally be able to prove that those elements differ from their European inspiration so deeply, and constitute a new configuration and new quality that might be called "Latin American positivism".

## EUROPEAN CORE

Drawing a picture of European positivism as a coherent movement might also be deceiving and oversimplifying; it has many national variations and even within "national" versions of positivism, there was an overwhelming multiplicity of thinkers and philosophers. As Ardao accurately notices, French and English positivism had the strongest influence on Latin America; we therefore focus on these two. However, as Ardao further explains that positivism was not a solid, coherent movement in France nor in England: "we shall find

---

[83] M. I. Clark, *The Emergence and Transformation of Positivism*, [in:] S. Nuccetelli, O. Schutte, O. Bueno, *A Companion to Latin American Philosophy*, Malden, Maryland, Wiley-Blackwell, 2010, p. 57.

out that positivism in each [of those countries – M. M.] is not the same, but that within each country, positivism is open to many different interpretations. In France, there have been many interpretations of positivism, from that of its creator, Comte, to that of Taine, and many others, such as: Littré, Laffitte, Renan, et al. In England, positivism varied from John Stuart Mill to Spencer, and, we might add Darwin, Bain, Huxley"[84].

Despite this complexity of inspiration we will concentrate on two leading figures: August Comte among French positivists and Herbert Spencer[85] among the English one. But we should not neglect the earlier inspiration. We might trace the origins of positivism in Jeremy Bentham's utilitarian ethics, as well as in the writings of Henri de Saint Simon. The impact, of the latter on the intellectual development of young Comte is indisputable[86]. Saint Simon pioneering investigations concerned principally with the establishment of the scientific study of man and society, what he called "social physiology". This social physiology can be perceived as one of the first

---

[84] A. Ardao, *op. cit.*, p. 515.

[85] Although John Stuart Mill played tremendous role in the dissemination of Comtean philosophy in England, just to mention his magnificent book *Auguste Comte and Positivism* published in 1866 in London we should remember that, Mill was not mere Comte's follower, and there are many moments where they are completely different. For example, Mill's ethical system is based on utility principle, while, according to Mill, Comte lacks any principles at all. As Mill wrote: "the error which is often, but falsely, charged against the whole class of utilitarian moralists; he required that the test of conduct should also be the exclusive motive of it. (...) M. Comte is a morality-intoxicated man. Every question with him is one of morality, and no motive but that of morality is permitted". J. S. Mill, *Auguste Comte and Positivism*, [in:] i d e m, *Collected Works of John Stuart Mill*, Vol. 32, Toronto, University of Toronto Press, 1991, pp. 335-336. Also from Latin American perspective the impact of Mill was minor compared to what extent Comte and Spencer shaped Latin American thought.

[86] Cf. M. Pickering, *Auguste Comte: An Intellectual Biography*, Cambridge, Cambridge University Press, 1993, pp. 60-139.

pre-positivist inspirations. Saint Simon was also the first to use the term positivism. Apart from his groundbreaking role in originating positivism he had a direct impact on many Latin American thinkers. The most appealing for Latin American independentists were his utopian socialist postulates combined with the belief that in course of social development, the old ruling classes must be replaced by the new classes of intellectuals, scientists, engineers and industrialists. The thinker that was mostly fascinated by such socialist ideas of Saint Simone was Argentine, Esteban Echeverría (1805-1851). The influence of Saint Simon's philosophy is visible from the early 1830s. But his *El Dogma Socialista* (Socialist Dogma) from 1846 is the fullest exposition of Simon's utopianism.

Nevertheless, Comte as the core figure of the positivist movement played a formative role in the development of positivism in both: Europe and Latin America. His personal ties and relations with the entire generation of Latin American positivists have been very well documented[87]. In his six volumes of *Cours de philosophie positive* (1830–1842), he presented his most widely known set of ideas. He based his theory on the studies of human intelligence through time, and identified three stages of human thought and human development. "The law is this: that each of our leading conceptions, — each branch of our knowledge, — passes successively through three different theoretical conditions: the Theological, or fictitious; the Metaphysical, or abstract; and the Scientific, or positive. (…) Hence arise three philosophies, or general systems of conceptions on the aggregate of phenomena, each of which excludes the others. The first is the necessary point of departure of the human understanding; and the third is its fixed and definitive state. The second is

---

[87] His personal ties with the entire generation of future positivists are very well documented. Cf. M. Pickering, *Auguste Comte: An Intellectual Biography*, Vol. 3, Cambridge, CUP, 2009, pp. 575-577.

merely a state of transition"[88]. As Comte said, the two previous stages are transitional, and the final, culminating stage of human progress would be the positive state, in which the empirical and scientific explanation would replace the explanatory role of metaphysical and supernatural entities.

Comte codified a new scientific method. According to his *Positive Philosophy*: "Reasoning and observation, duly combined, are the means of this knowledge. What is now understood when we speak of an explanation of facts is simply the establishment of a connection between single phenomena and some general facts, the number of which continually diminishes with the progress of science"[89]. That is the most concise definition of the positive method, the method that is based on the observation and generalization of conclusions. Consequently, this method would lead to the creation of coherent explanatory structure of laws and principles[90].

In his later work *Systéme de politique positive* (System of Positive Polity) (1851-4) he also studied the "social dynamics", to ground science and progress of religious and political systems. The progress for Comte was an inevitable part of human development. The consequence of progress will be the fact that the society must finally reach the third, positive stage of development. Progress has been identified with the positive stage of development. As Comte wrote: "The one great conception which belongs to this third phase is that of human progress, as an express view"[91]. Progress along with order became the leading terms of Comtean philosophy.

---

[88] A. Comte, M. Harriet, *The Positive Philosophy*, New York, AMS Press, 1974, pp. 1-2.

[89] *Ibidem*.

[90] A. Comte, *The Positive Philosophy of Auguste Comte*, trans. H. Martineau, Vol. 3, London, G. Bell & Sons, 1896, pp. 352-354.

[91] *Ibidem*, p. 270.

The last milestone of Comtean philosophy was the idea of positive religion, or the "religion of humanity". In the new religion, the society would develop moral qualities under the guidance of sociologist-priests, with ceremonies reminiscent of those of Catholicism. Comte more deeply elaborates this theory in *Instituting the Religion of Humanity*, (1851-1854, four volumes). The theory was controversial and after Comte's death, led to a schism within the positivists movement. Pierre Laffitté literary followed this concept while Émile Littré rejected the idea of positive religion as inconsistent with the non-idealistic foundation expressed by Comte in his earlier period. Both, Laffitté and Littré made an impact on Latin American thinkers.

Among English positivists, it was Herbert Spencer, not Mill, who made a tremendous impact on Latin American thinkers. The most appealing for them were those elements that preceded Darwinian evolutionary theory incorporated into Spencer's system.

In his first and one of the most influential books, *Social Statics,* published in 1851, Spencer presented his theory of the evolutionary progress of humanity merged with the organicist model of society: "Progress, therefore, is not an accident, but a necessity. (...) The modifications mankind have undergone, and are still undergoing, result from a law underlying the whole organic creation; and provided the human race continues, and the constitution of things remains the same, those modifications must end in completeness. As surely as the tree becomes bulky when it stands alone, and slender if one of a group, (...) so surely must things be called evil and immoral disappear; so surely must man become perfect"[92].

His concept of evolutionary progress was elaborated further in the essay *Progress: its Law and Cause* written in 1857 where he

---

[92]  H. Spencer, *Social Statics or the Conditions Essential to Happiness Specified and the First of them Developed*, London, John Chapman, 1851, p. 65.

presented progress as an inevitable process and transition from simple homogeneous structures into heterogeneous ones[93]. This evolutionary approach was applied in *Synthetic Philosophy* also toward social phenomena. Even though Spencer, during his lifetime, was rarely perceived as a social Darwinist, and his evolutionism preceded Darwin's ideas (the first trace of Spencer's evolutionism might be found in *Social Statics* dated from 1851, while *On the Origin of Species* was published in 1859), there are strong ties between the Spencerian system and social Darwinism[94]. Spencer rephrased Darwin's term "natural selection" into the "survival of the fittest"[95]. In *Principles of Biology*, Spencer expressed his faith that only those who are the most successfully adapted, will survive and pass their better intellectual and biological qualities to the offspring. There is no room for altruism an a society that competes for limited resources. Those who are not adapted to the natural and social challenge should be left alone.

## LATIN AMERICAN POSITIVISM – WHAT TO PICK UP AND WHY?

In tracing the difference between Latin American positivism and its European inspiration, we identified four elements that we intend to elaborate on more extensively. We believe that they are distinct for Latin American positivism and can be found in any of the Latin American countries:

- Positivism treated as a tool for a greater goal,
- Racial issues,

---

[93] Idem, *Essays: Scientific, Political and Speculative*, Vol. 1, London, Williams & Norgate, 1891, pp. 9, 38.

[94] The existence correspondence between Spencer and Darwin proves that they were familiar with each other's works.

[95] Idem, *Principles of Biology*, Vol. 1, London, Williams & Norgate, 1864, pp. 444-445.

- Emphasis on order,
- Hyper-importance of education.

## POSITIVISM TREATED AS A TOOL FOR A GREATER GOOD

There are few elements that are distinct for Latin American positivism. The first and most important one is the reason why positivism
in Latin America was so enthusiastically welcomed. Positivism was
welcomed so enthusiastically because it provided instruments for
the higher and the greater good – the creation of a new society in
the new republics. The common diagnosis was that Latin American
societies and states did not reach the final stage of development.
Positivism offered a tool and explanation as to how to achieve this.
This instrumental approach toward positivism was like the meta-
factor that directly or indirectly caused all the remaining differences.

The first five decades after the eruption of the wars for independence in Latin America were a hard time for the former European
colonies in the New World. The newly established sovereign states
were, for a long time, looking for a proper model of a political system, economic strategy and a proper construction of their complicated societies. In effect, the first decades of independence was
a time of long-lasting turmoil, civil wars, economic troubles and
social clashes. Also, it was the time of endless disputes between two
large factions, liberals on the one hand and conservatives on the
other. Their programs were completely different, which resulted in
endless conflicts. Those two factions and conflicts between them
were present in almost all the countries of Latin America. In this
situation, the region was perceived as very unstable and unfriendly
for any modernizing attempts. This does not, however, mean that
there were no attempts or no groups that did not think about creating stable conditions for the development of their particular states

or Latin America as an entire region. In fact, both liberals and conservatives presented two different concepts of building strong, modern and attractive states. The core problem was that the ideas were completely different and there was almost no place for compromise. As liberals demanded civil liberties and free trade, conservatives saw the domination of government over the citizens and protectionism in the trade as foundations of the new order. While liberals were talking about the separation of church and state or were condemning slavery, conservatives perceived them as essential elements of the post-colonial system. In this situation, it was very hard to solve conflicts between those two factions. In some countries it was easier, as for example in Costa Rica, Chile or Brazil, but there was a great majority of Latin American young republics that sunk in chaos, such as: Mexico, Colombia or Argentina, to name but a few.

The situation started to change at the beginning of the second half of the nineteenth century. There were several reasons for that change. In general, on could observe liberals taking power in one country after another. That created friendly conditions for economic development and political stability. After years of political conflicts and civil wars, Latin American societies were tired and were looking for stability, peace, and economic development. A change in political and intellectual elites in Latin America could also be observed. The new generation came to power. The fathers of independence were gone and the next generation had different views of the world, progress, and societies among in which they lived. A lot of those new elites were educated in European universities. As it was in the pastt, young Latin American elites educated in Europe brought new ideas to the New World with them. As the second half of the 19th century was the time of the triumph of positivism in Europe, it quickly came to Latin America. Positivist philosophy found very favorable conditions. A common desire for order and progress resulted in the main ideas of positivist thinking being very attractive for Latin American intellectuals that were looking for solutions to problems of their countries as well as the entire continent. Bringing ideas of Comte and Spencer was very popular in the second half of the 19th century in Latin America. It is necessary to point out, in accordance with Arturo Ardao, that it was not only the simple import of positivist philosophy. "It was not only adopted but adapted" wrote Ardao[96]. Many Latin Americans were fascinated with positivist thought; many believed that the solutions proposed by representatives of European positivism would be able to resolve the problems of young Latin American republics. However, they were also conscious of the peculiarity that their particular states presented as well as the entire region. The simple adoption of European ideas would not solve problems that encumbered those states. Although the ideas of Comte or Spencer can truly aspire to the name of the complete philosophical system, it was created in a different political, social, economic and cultural condition. It aimed to resolve different problems and based on different foundations. As Latin American countries were politically unstable, economically underdeveloped, socially complicated and culturally different, the positivist ideas had to function in different conditions than in Europe. Also, there were different problems to be resolved. The specific characteristics of Latin America, and even particular states in that region was noticed by Latin American positivist thinkers. Argentinean political theorist – Juan Bautista Alberdi – wrote in 1842 – about the differences between Europe and New World, and he underlined that positivist philosophy in Latin America had to consider her problems and necessities. "Our philosophy, then, has to emerge from our necessities. What are, according to those necessities, issues that America should define and resolve immediately? It is freedom, law, and social advantages that allow man to enjoy social and political order. It is also the issue of social

---

[96] A. Ardao, *op. cit.*, p. 515.

organization in the most proper way in the aim of improving human nature on American soil. Hence, American philosophy should basically be political and social in its subject, fervent and prophetic in its instincts, synthetic and organic in its method, positivist and realist in its procedures, and republican in its spirit and goals"[97].

Representatives of Latin American positivist intelligentsia understood pretty well that the simple adoption of European thought is not enough. Moreover, just the adoption of positivist ideas in Latin America would not be proper. It can be stated that in those times, Latin American societies were much more complicated than European ones. Class divisions and racial, ethnic, social, cultural etc divisions were also present. This is why some aspects of European positivist thought were accented more strongly in Latin America than in Europe. For example, racial problems, the case of political stability, economic development or education were probably more important for Latin Americans than for a majority of citizens in European countries. Solutions proposed by Latin American positivists sometimes varied from those proposed by Europeans and they did not restrain themselves from the free interpretations of European ideas[98]. It should not to be a surprise, then, that the case of race, political and economic order and education are the most important subjects of positivist thought in Latin American countries. It is also

---

[97] "Nuestra filosofía, pues, ha de salir de nuestras necesidades. Pues según estas necesidades, cuáles son os problemas que la America está llamada a establecer y resolver en estos momentos? – Son lo de la libertad, de los derechos y goces sociales de que el hombre puede disfrutar en el mas alto grado en el orden social y politico; son los de la organización pública mas adecuada a las exigencias de la naturaleza perfectible del hombre, en el suelo americano. De aqui es que la filosofía americana debe se esencialmente política y social en su objeto, ardiente y profética en sus instinctos, sintética y orgánica en su método, positivista y realista en sus procederes, republicana en su espíritu y destinos". J. B. Alberdi, *Ideas para presidir a la conferención del curso de filosofía contemporánea*, [in:] L. Zea (ed.), *op. cit.*, pp. 65-66.
[98] G. Horváth, S. Szabó, *op. cit.*

necessary to say that those subjects are closely connected to each other. The question of relations between different races was closely related to the social order. Due to the large scale of illiteracy in Latin American societies, the case of education was extremely important. The development of those countries depended on the development of education; also, the nation-building process was very closely related with race and education. The matter of political order was connected to all the cases mentioned above. As Latin American positivists fully accepted the motto "order and progress", they had to defy those subjects.

## RACIAL ISSUES

Searching for an explanation of social backwardness, some Latin American intellectuals found them in the racial structure, created as the consequence of inferiority of racial mixtures with indigenous and black people. Therefore, they took Spencer's theory of evolution and adapted it to the racial issues. Common assumptions about the cultural inferiority of indigenous people were shared by many, and indigenous people were perceived as the obstacle element toward progress. This racial considerations introduced to Latin American positivism created the next element, unique for Latin American positivism, and not present in the European one.

The interlink between the case of race and progress and modernity was not easy to resolve in Latin American societies. They were very different in that case. There were countries where the question about racial relations was not very urgent. Racial tensions were relatively low in countries such as: Argentina, Uruguay or even Chile. After years of conquest and later of colonial rule in those countries, symbolic numbers of indigenous people remained. There were also countries such as: Bolivia, Peru, Guatemala or Mexico where Indians were a significant part of society. For positivists, the question about the race and their connection with progress and modernity was clear. Europeans achieved the highest level of development in almost every field of human activity. This is why Europeans should lead other parts of the world toward progress. It was Domingo Faustino Sarmiento – Argentinean writer and politician – who paid closer attention to the racial relations in Argentina, but his reflections should be understood as a proposition for all Latin American republics. The specific characteristic of Argentina and most of the other Latin American countries was a small number of citizens. According to Sarmiento, that was one of the most important obstacles for development. His proposal for solving that problem was very clear: European immigration. According to him, it was European immigration that determined the success of the colonies in North America. He proposed that Argentina and other Latin American states should take up a strong effort to encourage Europeans to settle down in the New World. "Let's make the Republic of Argentina a homeland for all who leave Europe", appealed Sarmiento[99]. He believed that educated and hard-working European immigrants would not only help to populate the vast territories of Latin American states but that they would help implement the fundamental goal of all positivists, Latin American ones as well as European. "Those envoys should be hard working men that will study methods used by those nations [European nations – K. D.] with the purpose of self-fulfillment. They should communicate with people that we want to bring to our country because of their profession. Our embassies in Europe should be public offices that will deliver thousands of hard working emigrants to us, tempt males, bias European public opinion positively toward

---

[99] D. F. Sarmineto, *Agripolis o la capital de los estados confederados del Rio de la Plata*, [in:] L. Zea, *op. cit.*, p. 68.

our countries that are unknown [in Europe – K. D.] with the exception of wars and disorder"[100].

Sarmiento was not alone in those hopes located in European immigration to Latin America. He expected that immigration would create a domination of European civilization in the New World that would produce order and progress, while another Argentinean – Juan Bautista Alberdi – stated that European presence in Latin America was nothing new. Moreover, that presence could be perceived as a real blessing and an independent Latin America is a product of Europe. "South American Republics are the fruit and the live testimony of European activity in America. What is referred to as independent America it is nothing more than Europe established in America; our revolution is nothing else than the division of European power for two parts that are self-governing now"[101]. According to Alberdi, everything that is not European is barbarian. "In Latin America everything that is not European is barbarian: there is no other division than that: 1) indigenous – means – barbarians, 2) European – means – those who are born in America, speak Spanish and believe in Jesus Christ, not in Pillan"[102]. This kind of think-

---

[100] "Estos enviados debían ser hombres laoriosos, ocupados exclusivamente de estudiar los medios que aquellas naciones emplean para enriquecerse; de ponerse en contacto con los hombres que por su ciencia, su industria, nos convendría hacer venir a nuestro país. Nuestras embajadas en Europa deberían ser oficinas públicas, para procurarnos y enviarnos millares de emograntes laboriosos, para seducir hombres, para predisponer por la prenda la opinión de la Europa en favor de nuestros países, poco conocidos hasta hoym si no es por sus guerras y sus desórdenes", *ibidem*, p. 71.
[101] "Las Repúblicas de la America se Sur son producto y testimonio vivo de la acción de Europa en America. Lo que llamamos America independiente no es mas que Europa establecida en America; nuestra revolución no es otra cosa que la desmembración de un poder europeo en dos mitades, que hoy se manejan por sí mismas", J. B. Alberdi, *Bases y puntos...*, p. 79.
[102] "En America todo lo que es europeo es bárbaro: no hay mas división que ésta: 1) el indigena, es decir, el salvaje, 2) el europeo, es decir, nosotros los que hemos nacido en

ing was characteristic for a great majority of positivists in the New World. There was no place for indigenous communities in the idea of Latin America created on European resemblance. The only proposal for them was the adoption of European cultural patterns. As the main goal of all positivists was economic development, political order and social modernization, the old, often primitive in the eyes of all those fixed with European civilization predominance, indigenous communities were one of the obstacles toward modernity. Alcides Arguedas, Bolivian intellectual, paid attention in one of his essays to the conflict that still exists between indios and white people. "(…)A Native American (el indio) created by the routine dies in the routine and the effects of its efforts do not move the country forward because it is purely mechanic and it lacks a spark of intelligence, a conscious effort accomplished in the aim of social solidarity. Hence, there is no relationship or similarity between a Native American and a white man. They are two races that are living together but do not know each other. (…) The Native American sees an eternal enemy in the white man and he lives in fear of him and hates him, not to say despises him (…)"[103].

The reluctance of positivist elites toward indigenous communities in Latin American republics was specific and characteristic. It is

---

America y hablamos español, los que creemos en Jesucristo y no en Pillan", *ibidem*, p. 80.

[103] "El indio, creado en la rutina, muere rutinario y el producto de su esfuerzo no hace avanzar al país porque es puramente mecánico, si se quiere, y falta en esa actividad la chispa de la inteligencia cultivada, del esfuerzo consciente desplegado con fines de solidaridad social. (…) De ahí que entre el indio y el blanco no existe ninguna relación, ni afinidad. Son dos razas que, conviviendo, se ignoran profundamente. Nunca puso el ningún esfuerzo en conocer a fondo al indio para saber, al fin, qué podría obtener de él y hasta dónde podía contar con su colaboración consciente. El indio jamás vio en el blanco otra cosa que al enemigo hereditario y vive temiéndole y odiándole, por no decir despreciándole, a su manera", A. Arguedas, *La dictadura y la anarquia*, [in:] L. Zea, *Pensamiento positivista…*, p. 363.

interesting that those Argentinean, Mexican, Bolivian etc. intellectuals did not notice the richness of the indigenous culture. It will be less surprising if we remember the fundamental credo of all positivists in the world, especially of the New World: order and progress. According to them, the end justifies the means. Uneducated and poor masses of Indians could not ensure those goals. Moreover, they were perceived as an obstacle toward modernity and development. In this situation, it should be no surprise that the solution could be the Europeanization of Latin American societies. New governments that were dominated by positivists ideas, have taken a strong effort toward civilizing the indigenous population through Europeanization. The question was if those populations are capable of transforming into a modern style, meaning European. Governing elites decided that it is impossible not only in Mexico, but also in a large majority of other states with significant numbers of indigenous communities. In effect, Latin American governments adopted strongly anti-Indian programs. The most popular is the policy of Porfirio Díaz regime. In the name of modernity and development, Porfirio Díaz implemented a strongly anti-Indian policy[104]. As the territories that belonged to indigenous communities were necessary to build railways, it was very common to take away those territories. The Yaqui Indians affairs are one of the most significant cases of displacement of the entire community. The new elites were strongly convinced that the positivist thought, with its evidently anti-Indian and sometimes racist ideas, is the key to creating modern societies. One of the most brilliant positivist intellectuals from Chile strongly underlined that only the adoption of positivist ideas could help Latin American countries create modern societies. He maintained that positivist thought is the only creative one and that it is in the

---

[104] W. D. Raat, *Los intelectuales, el positivismo y la cuestión indígena*, "Historia Mexicana" 1971, Vol. 20, No. 3, pp. 414-415.

nature of positivist philosophy to serve the well-being of mankind. "Positivism, as you can see it, is not an act of negation, aggression, deconstruction; it is exclusively an act of affirmation, reconciliation, and creation"[105]. He invoked another positivist sentence for the confirmation of his thesis: Love, as a rule, order as a base, progress as an end. In his opinion, only the adoption of positivist ideas could bring Latin American societies progress and modernity. "Positivism is capable of reorganizing a modern society in a definite manner, as it is based on the most profound study of the previous social organism"[106].

## EMPHASIS ON ORDER

Progress and order in the Latin American version of positivism were inextricably bound together. Moreover, the implementation of order in any aspect: political, economic or social was treated as an indispensable condition for progress. Chaos and anarchy were major enemies for positivists. Consequently, order was often identified with political power and a government that was able to implement and sustain it. Therefore, Latin American positivism was sometimes much closer to a political ideology than to a philosophical movement. Also, the personal connections between the positivists and political power were very strong, many of them were members of parliament or the government.

---

[105] J. Lagarrigue, *Positivismo y catolicismo*, [in:] L. Zea, *Pensamiento positivista...*, p. 412; in the other place of the same text, Lagarrigue wrote: "The spirit of positivism is, besides, naturally creative, organic and confirms that in social order it is not destructive but replace", (El espíritu positivo es ademas, por naturaleza, esencialmente constructor, orgánico, y afirma que, en el orden social, no se destruye sino lo que se reemplaza), *ibidem*, p. 423.

[106] *Ibidem*, p. 420.

The *sine qua non* condition of progress was order for Latin Americans in general, not only for those who believed in positivist philosophy. It is impossible to achieve progress in terms of disorder, chaos, and conflict. That is why the positivists in Latin America paid extremely strong attention to with the aim of creating a stable and strong government. The founding fathers of European positivism perceived society in a biological way – for them society was a living organism. This thesis was broadly accepted among positivists in other parts of the world, also in Latin America. Justo Sierra – one of the most prominent and influential positivists in Mexico wrote then: "Scientific politics are based on biology applied to society", and further wrote Sierra "Public order does not consist of strength or energy of power but a consensus, a voluntary and spontaneous agreement of citizens to create order"[107]. As Herbert Spencer, Justo Sierra had described society as a "superorganism". "Society, as every organism, is subject to essential laws of evolution that in its basic part depend on a double move of integration and differentiation, the move from homogenic to heterogenic, from incoherent to coherent; in every organism during the process of unification or integration its parts differentiate and specialize, and this two–way move decides about the perfection of an organism, which in the case of society, it is called progress"[108].

---

[107] "Puesto que la política científica tiene por la base la biología aplicada a las sociedades y que a todo desarollo exagerado del cerebro corresponde el raquitismo del cuerpo social, a toda concentración vigorosa correspondería la anemia y la disolución del país, y en misma proporción que la concentración disminuya aumentará la robustez y la virillidad del cuerpo social. (…) el orden público no consiste en la fuerza o enrgía del poder, sino en el consensus, en la voluntaria y espontánea conformidad de los ciudadanos en realizar el orden", J. S i e r r a, *Sobre política nacional*, [in:] L. Z e a, *Pensamiento positivista…*, p. 179.

[108] "La sociedad, como todo organismo, está sujeto a las leyes necesarias de la evolución; que éstas en su parte esencial consisten en un doble movimiento de integración y de diferenciación, en una marcha de lo homogéneo a lo heterogéneo, de lo incoher-

The greatest and most visible distinction of positivist ideas in Latin America and Europe was the fact that different countries in the New World adopted different solutions in the political field. It is necessary to remember that European positivists spoke in the same way in the field of political affairs, however, there were some subtle but important differences. Spencer or Comte had the same goal – political order, but the means to reach the end varied. Different solutions were adopted in particular states of Latin America, sometimes they were closer to Spencer's thought other times heavily inspired by Comte or Mill. For example, Argentina adopted solutions that were based on the political thought of Spencer, Brazil was close to Comte, and Mexico was trying to find its own way by mixing both of them[109]. Latin American intellectuals very often combined ideas that are commonly known as liberal – as for example a republican form of government – with propositions suggested by positivism, among which the most important is the concept of *'política científica'*. The concept is based on the thesis that scientific methods could be used in resolving national problems. Positivist intellectuals perceived politics as an 'experimental science' that is based on facts[110]. What is specific for Latin American nations, it is the tendency towards authoritarian governance. In effect, at the end of the nineteenth century, there was a large majority of Latin American countries that had an undemocratic form of government. One of the most explicit examples of that specific Latin American combination of liberal and positivists ideas was Mexico during the Porfirio Díaz regime be-

---

ente a lo coherente, que en todo organismo, a medida que se unifica o se integra mas, sus partes mas se diferencian, mas se especializan, y en este doble movimiento consiste el perfeccionamiento del organismo, lo que en las sociedades se llama progreso", *ibidem*, p. 180.

[109] A. Ardao, *op. cit.*, p. 519.

[110] *Historia de América Latina*, Vol. 8: *América Latina. Cultura y sociedad, 1870-1930*, Barcelona, Cambridge University Press, 1986, p. 18.

tween 1876 and 1910. The republican and democratic form of rule have formally been preserved there. But in practice, it was a strongly undemocratic regime that was based on positivist thought. Porfirio Díaz created a very hermetic group of advisers. The group – called Sientificos – was trying to enforce the most important elements of positivist views on political order. This was the group of graduate students, teachers, professors, journalists, and poets. In its ideas, this young group did not differentiate a lot from the old liberal slogans that had been introduced since the fall of the empire. As it seems, the group was inclined more toward conservatism, oligarchy and technocracy then the old liberal guard. It was positivist, apart from several exceptions[111]. As wrote Arturo Ardao, porfirism and positivism became one in Mexico[112]. Mexican positivists used some of the ideas proposed by different European philosophers and create a unique political system. It should not be a surprise that the system of Porfiriato was sometimes called a perfect dictatorship. Justo Sierra – one of the leaders of the Scientificos in Mexico – described their attitude toward the right to elect government in these words: We are not the enemies of democracy; of course, it is not our ideal type of government; we will always prefer the rule of science, reason, of people that create the spirit of the country, in opposition to the rule of the crowd, power, matter; but the biggest danger would be the belief in the possibility of approximation to universal suffrage in our age and in the frame of our election law[113].

---

[111] E. Velásquez García, *Nueva historia general de México*, Mexico City, Colegio de México, 2011, p. 674.

[112] A. Ardao, *op. cit.*, p. 520.

[113] "No somos enemigos de la democracia; no es por cierto nuestro ideal de gobierno; le preferiremos siempre el de la ciencia, el de razón, el de los hombres que compnen el elemento espiritual de un país, en contraposición del de las multitudes, que es la fuerza, que es el número, que es la matria; pero nada habría mas peligroso que creer

Describing a completely different reality that took place in Colombia, one of the Colombian intellectuals emphasized the link between political order on the one hand and the economic and social progress on the other hand. This correlation was present in all Latin American states. Although the problems of order and progress were common for all those states, the solutions chosen by them were different. This also creates a specific characteristic of Latin American positivism – derived from a common foundation which was positivist philosophy and aiming toward the same goals, Latin Americans could produce their own, original solutions. They had the same origins of tradition and history but the political forms they had adopted after independence and later in the last decades of the 19th century were different[114].

## HYPER-IMPORTANCE OF EDUCATION

Educational issues were another distinctive feature of Latin American positivism. Intellectuals attached great importance to the issue of education. The main attempt was to create a new, post-colonial class of lawyers, doctors, mathematicians, and other scientists who would constitute the new elite of the society. The traditional universities, academies and professional institutes were inadequate for this task. Most of them were created during the colonial period and education in those institutions was often conducted under the auspices of the Church. The process of acquiring knowledge was rather based on memorizing information rather than on observing and analyzing. Therefore, Latin American positivists took part in one of

posile en nuestra época y en nuestro syfragio efectivo, se acercase sin cesar al sufragio universal", J. Sierra, *op. cit.*, p. 185.

[114] R. Nuñez, *La reforma politica en Colombia*, [in:] L. Zea, *Pensamiento positivista...*, Vol. 2, pp. 243-244.

the greatest attempts of reform – to completely and totally re-shape the system of public education, and sometimes even build it from the ground up. It is not that European positivists did not pay attention to the educational issues, but in Latin America, the importance of educational reform was hyperbolized to the extreme.

The subject of education is closely connected with aims such as modernity, progress and order. The belief in science was one of the foundations for positivist thought. The conviction in human reasoning and the superiority of that what is rational over everything that is based on belief was common for all positivists. For them, everything could be explained as the result of scientific theories. For this reason, one of the most significant products of the positivist thought is sociology – a science that investigates processes and phenomenon that take place in society. Especially for those who wanted to build a completely new order in Latin American states, the science over the society – sociology – was a very important instrument and very important source of knowledge about their nations. "The new science that, through the social tendencies of humans, refers to the laws that manage the historical development of common beings, called nations. Sociology, is the new branch of philosophy that the powerful intelligence that was only able to be seen by the Greeks of the times of the Marathon. [Philosophy – K. D.], through empirical procedure, and the exclusion of errors, gave the Roman Empire the possibility of achieving great progress in the age of its astonishing development. Philosophy that practically since the first century began to occupy appropriate dimension and place in the hierarchy of social sciences"[115]. The new discipline of science – sociology – was

---

[115] "Una nueva sciencia (…) la que se refiere a las leyes que, por medio de las tendencias sociales del hombre, presiden desarrollo histórico de los seres colectivos llamados naciones: de la Sociologia, esa nueva rama de la Filosofia que la poderosa inteligencia de los griegos del siglo de Maratón apenas alcanzó a vislumbrar; en la que por un procedimiento empírico, y por lo tanto expuesto a error dio grandes pasos el pueblo

of great importance for all positivists. But it is still important to remember the Latin American context. The period of the second half of the 19th century was the time of nation building for those republics. It was that period when national identity emerged. The citizens of Perú, Mexico, Colombia or other states started to think about themselves in first order as: Peruvians, Mexicans or Colombians and as creols, Aymara, metis etc. in second order. That is why the birth of sociology was very important for all Latin Americans positivists. That permitted them to find solutions for problems that were present among the Latin American nations.

The birth of sociology was important and had a huge significance for positivists in general, especially for those from Latin America. The most important goal for them was to establish order and progress. This was impossible in the societies were the great majority of people were uneducated or their education was very poor. That is why Latin American positivist intellectuals paid great attention to the development of education, especially higher education with the priority of science over humanities disciplines. The words of José Ingenieros – another of the great Argentinean positivists, provide such an attitude. He saw the aim of schools in teaching useful skills. "The school's predominant goal is to unveil that an activity is pleasant when it is applied to the profits"[116]. Positivists, also those from the New World, all were strong enthusiasts of creating a social reality. They were convinced that it is possible to formulate rules that direct different processes in societies, and that fact could be used to regulate phenomenon that take place inside the particular

---

romano en las épocas de su asombrosa virillidad, y que sólo de un siglo a esta parte empieza a tomar número y lugar determinado en la jerarquía de las ciencias sociales", S. Camacho Roldán, *El estudio sobre la sociolgía*, [in:] L. Zea, *Pensamiento positivista...*, Vol. 2, p. 211.

[116] J. Ingenieros, *Educación, escuela, maestro*, [in:] L. Zea, *Pensamiento positivista...*, Vol. 2, p. 165.

society. Education was, in this situation, extremely important as it could research and teach those rules and then could be used to solve the problems of those societies. "Education, (...), is nothing more than an intervention in the process of adaptation of an individual to the surrounding world and society to facilitate and guide it in the aim of creation of situation in which the inevitable law of selection is changing itself in the instrument of an individual and collective evolution"[117], wrote Cuban positivist, Enrique José Varona. But for Latin Americans, the role of education has not been restricted to innovations and usefulness. Latin American positivists saw the huge task of education which played a great role in creating a national identity. Justo Sierra who was largely engaged in reforming the system of higher education in Mexico, very strongly underlined the necessity of active participation of universities in creating or reinforcing national identity. "It's about the University that would be the crowning factor of a great composition of national education. (...) At every primary school, at every Mexican school there is nation who learns, it learns in groups but in fact the entire nation learns. National education integrates, it creates nation's life"[118].

Positivists paid strong attention to science and education. It was common in Europe as well as in Latin America. But the purposes for which both had to serve were specific. That was the consequence of the specific characteristics of Latin American societies. Nearly fifty

---

[117] "Educar, desde un punto de vista comprensivo, no es nada menos que intervenir en la adaptación del individuo al mundo cirunstante y a la sociedad, facilitarla y dirigirla, para procurar que la ineludible ley de selección se convierta en instrumento de progreso personal y colectivo", E. J. Varona, *Sobre la educiación*, [in:] *ibidem*, p. 54.

[118] "Se trata de una Universidad que sea el coronamiento de una grande obra de educación nacional. (...) En cada escuela primaria, en cada escuela mexicana se educa a la nación, se educa en porciones, pero se educa a la nación entera en todas ellas; (...) la educación nacional integra la hace la vida de la nación", J. Sierra, *Iniciativa para crear la universidad*, [in:] *ibidem*, p. 78.

years after gaining independence, Latin American nations were still in the phase of creation. Education had, in this situation, a very important task – to help in building a national identity, and *ipso facto*, in creating modern nation states.

The same concerned other elements of positivist thought. Every idea that was imported to Latin America was reformulated. This reformulation was enforced by specific conditions that existed in particular states in the region. Since the problems of particular republics were very often of completely different nature than those in European countries, the European ideas had to be transformed to adapt to the local necessities. It is undisputed that a huge positivist impact on Latin American elites took place in the second half of the 19th century. It was also true that specific, Latin American positivism existed that was based on the thought of Comte, Spencer, and others Europeans, but it created its own characteristics, as well.

***

Positivism in Latin America developed as a response to the intellectual needs of the Continent: the fight against colonial heritage, the need for establishing a new, independent identity on both a continental and a national level. Such an instrumental attitude resulted in acquiring only those elements from European positivism that were connected with the needs of newly established republics, mostly creating a new society, sharing a new identity. The approach of Latin American thinkers is reflected in Alberdi's claim that "our philosophy, then, has to emerge from our necessities".

The intellectuals knew that Latin America was underdeveloped as compared to Europe, therefore, they accepted the law of three stages of development with great optimism. They believed that very soon they would be able to achieve the final, most desired stage – the positive one. As Clark observed: "Many positivists believed that state-directed education and immigration would ameliorate the social and racial "degeneration" inherited from the colonial era"[119]. Such an attitude outlined two possible ways of modernizing the continent. Some of the Latin American positivists, inspired by Comte, considered education to be the driving force of change, even to a greater extent than European philosophers. The education was to create a social reality. Therefore, this group was named the social positivists. Education was not only a means to achieve the final, positive stage of development, but it should also create a new society, with new elites that would be prepared to govern the new republics.

Some other Latin American positivists blamed racial degeneration (mostly mestizos and mulattoes) to be the main reason for backwardness and they thought that progress could only be achieved by changing the racial structure of the continent. Therefore, they called for new wave of migration, by inviting European settlers. Philosophers of this group shared Spencer's vision of evolution, therefore, they were named evolutionary positivists. With their attitude, nationalism and some forms of racism became part of Latin American positivism.

Comte's vision of progress and order were adopted to the Latin American demands. And the order was perceived as the inevitable element of progress. That was a very practical attitude: they wanted to prevent revolution and to strengthen the legal government. Latin American positivists were quite often active members of the government. The emphasis on order and governance, along with their political activity, made Latin American positivism more like ideology than political philosophy.

Some key elements of European positivism were not included into the Latin American version. One of such elements was Comte's idea of the "religion of humanity". It had followers in Brazil (that was

---

[119] M. I. Clark, *The Emergence and Transformation of Positivism*, [in:] S. Nuccetelli, O. Schutte, O. Bueno, *op. cit.*, p. 59.

the only place in the world where it was practiced as a religion) but it also had several followers in Mexico (Agustin Aragon, Porfirio Parra).

From the very beginning, the Latin American intellectuals did not copy European positivism, they used it as the inspiration for a new, transformed and reinterpreted version of positivism. Latin American positivism was not only the adaptation of European thought, it was also developed independently from European inspirations. The best example of such an attitude is Lastarria saying: "(…) we were not familiar with any writer at all who had thought as we did; and even thought at that time [in 1844 – M. M.] August Comte was finishing the publication of his *Course de Philosophie Positive*, we had neither the remotest notice of the name of this illustrious philosopher nor his book, nor of his system of history, which was the same as ours"[120]. As Zea pointed out himself: "Positivism thus was already in the minds of the Hispanic-American thinkers, and when they discovered it, they readily assimilated it"[121].

There is still a question whether all these differences makes positivism in Latin America something special: Latin American positivism. We think that the answer is positive. Nuccetelli explains that "A philosophical theory is *characteristically* Latin American if and only if:
1) It offers original philosophical arguments, and
2) Its philosophical topics are in part determined by the relation its proponent bears to social and/or historical factors in Latin America"[122].

---

[120] J. V. Lastarria, *Recuerdos literarios. Datos para la historia literaria de la América española i del progreso intelectual en Chile*, Santiago de Chile, M. Servat, 1885, p. 250, translated by L. Zea, *The Latin-American Mind*, Norman, University of Oklahoma Press, 1963, p. 130. Emphasis added by the authors of this article.
[121] L. Zea, *The Latin-American…*, p. 131.
[122] S. Nuccetelli, *Latin American Thought…*, p. 246.

We hope that we proven that the second condition was achieved. But the first one still remains questionable. Latin American positivism, because of the connections with praxis and real problems of the societies, was less philosophical, less interested in abstract speculation: it was interested in practical solutions. The conclusion of Coriolano Alberini seems to be astonishingly right, when he claims that Latin American positivism is an example of anti-inspiration of Comte and Spencer: "first, because it neglects the fundamental problems of philosophy, and secondly, because it repudiates – at least in theory – all metaphysical preoccupations, professing instead a vague spirit of agnosticism"[123]. The opinion of Risieri Frondizi is quite similar because he states "that philosophy has been subordinated to non-philosophical interests". And further explains "Ibero-America added the narrowness which accrues to a theoretical system when it adheres to a program of action, when it becomes an instrument of activities alien to philosophy. (…) Ibero-America then had many practical, political, economic, and educational problems so urgent that it could not afford the luxury of disinterested reflection"[124]. Paradoxically, the non-philosophical nature of Latin American positivism is probably its most characteristic feature.

---

[123] C. Alberini, *Contemporary Philosophic Tendencies in South America, With Special Reference to Argentina,* "Monist" 1927, Vol. 37, No. 3, p. 329.
[124] *Ibidem,* p. 349.

DOI: 10.12797/9788376386775.04

# III. ANARCHISM IN MEXICO – DISTINCTION OR INNOVATION

# THE SPECIAL CASE OF MEXICAN ANARCHISM

The second half of the 19th century was a period of dynamic development of different philosophic and ideological reflections in the Latin American and Caribbean region. This is quite logical. After the first decades since their independence, Latin American countries were concentrated on strengthening their sovereignty and statehood. The process lasted in particular countries more or less time, however, about the mid-19th century the process of formation of independent states was completed in a majority of the Latin American republics. It started the period of the great interest of Latin American elites in different philosophic trends, mostly imported from Europe. The popularity of positivism among Latin American elites is a great example of this situation. Although, as it was explained in earlier fragments of this book, the application of European thoughts and ideas was not just a simple adoption. It was strongly filtered by the reality and peculiarity of the region. Ideas that were brought to Latin America from Europe were reinterpreted and adopted to the Latin American conditions. The second half of the 19th century was the time of significant migration from Europe to different Latin American countries. It was an important factor that facilitated the movement of ideas born in Europe. European migration to Latin American countries, among others, had a strong economic basis. Masses of poor inhabitants from European countries decided to leave their homes and look for a better life in the New World. The peasantry had a chance to get their own farm on the endless terrains in Latin American countries. Those who wanted to live in cities could count on a job in the emerging industry. As in mid-19th century Europe, numerous , more or less radical, ideologies were often discussed. European migrants were taking their views and ideas with them to Latin America. That is how the new ideologies appeared in Latin America in the second half of the 19th century.

Anarchism was among these, ideologies that appeared in Latin American in the mid-19th century. It was an example of the radical thought that was already quite popular in some European countries and was also gaining popularity in Latin American republics. It was the effect of the above-mentioned factors, however, there were also some internal conditions that were conducive to the spreading of anarchism in some of the countries of the region. First of all, the appearance of anarchism coincided with the growing process of industrialization. Taking power by liberals in almost all Latin American countries brought about significant changes in the economic policy. Industrialization was one of the principal elements of the liberal economic policy. As there was a chronic lack of economic sources and a highly skilled labor force, the only form of industrialization was an invitation of foreign investors to create their factories and new mines in particular countries of Latin America. As the process was initiated, the group of workers grew simultaneously with the growing industry. The group was dominated by local labor force but there was also a significant number of recent immigrants from Europe. Those immigrants mostly already had a strict ideological profile. This was the easiest way how radical ideologies originating in Europe were gaining popularity among the citizens of Latin American countries. This coincidence of several factors resulted in the emergence – as early as the 1870s – of anarchist groups in such

Latin American countries as: Argentina, Mexico, Cuba and Uruguay. Representatives of anarchist groups from these countries were present at the International Anarchist Congress in 1877. For the last quarter of the 19th century, the most active anarchist intellectuals and groups functioned in Argentina. Vivid anarchist activity in this country should not be any surprise. It was Argentina where thousands of emigrants from South Europe settled. They were the ones who actively promoted anarchist ideas. Ettore Mattei, an Italian immigrant, founded the *Circolo Comunista – Anarchico* in Buenos Aires in 1884, meanwhile another Italian anarchist – Errico Malatesta – published a bilingual Spanish – Italian journal entitled *La Questione Sociale*[125]. The anarchist movement was quite strong in the last years of the 19th-century and one could observe a tendency toward its further organization. As the movement was dominated by the anarcho – syndicalists, favorable conditions to base the struggle on the syndicalist movement appeeared. Pietro Gori was among the most important representatives of this tendency. Already in 1901, he was among the principal organizers of the Workers Federation of Argentina (*Federación Obrera Argenitna* – FOA). It was a significant success of the anarchist activists that strongly tended to create some kind of organization that would represent masses of workers. At this occasion, it was easy to observe a firm struggle between anarchists and Marxists. The latter ones were a small minority and in a short time had left the FOA[126]. At the FOA's congress in 1904, it changed its name to Workers Regional Federation of Argentina (*Federación Obrera Regional Argentina* – FORA). During the first decade of the 20th century, it was the most important workers organization in Argentina. It also had a significant impact on workers' anarchist move-

---

[125] M. Jorrín, J. D. Martz, *Latin American Political Thought and Ideology*, Chapel Hill, University of North Carolina Press, 1970, p. 187.

[126] A. J. Cappelletti, *Prologo*, [in:] C. M. Rama, A. J. Cappelletti, *El anarquismo en América Latina*, Caracas, Venezuela, Biblioteca Ayacucho, 1990, p. XXIV.

ments in other countries of the region. After the first decade of the 20th century, a difficult time arose for workers' movements in Argentina in general. It also included anarchist organizations. However, new periodicals that were promoting anarchist or socialist ideas, were still being developed. Also, strikes were the principal tool of workers struggle with government and private capitalists.

As the example of the anarchist movement in Argentina shows, the influence of European immigrants on the development of anarchist ideas in Latin America was undoubted, some characteristics that were particular for Latin American anarchists can also be observed. These particularities can lead to the thesis, that although anarchism in Latin America came from Europe and the anarchist movement was initiated in majority by European immigrants, there are some distinctions between the anarchist ideas developed in Europe and those that evolved in Latin America. These particularities and distinctions in the development of the anarchist movement between Europe and Latin America are perfectly visible in the case of Mexico. As the aim of the book is defining Latin American thought in the sense of its special characteristics, the we have deemed concentrating on the development of anarchism in Mexico as appropriate. This is also justified by the fact that Mexico is one of the Latin American countries where anarchist ideas and movements have been present in public discourse and played a significant role in Mexican politics. The specific situation of Mexican state in the second half of the 19th century resulted in the slow development of the anarchist movement. However, its leader and the most influential promoter – Ricardo Flores Magón – played a significant role in mobilizing Mexican society toward the rejection of the Porfirio Díaz regime and initiating a revolution. As it turned out, the Mexican revolution that erupted in the end of 1910 was the first great revolution in the 20th century, not only in the Latin American region but in general.

The social, political and economic situation in Mexico in the second half of 19th century was conducive to the appearance of radical ideologies. After the bloody War of the Reform between the liberals and conservatives at the turn of the 1850s and 1860s, a military intervention of European powers also took place. As Great Britain and Spain withdraw their forces from Mexico after a short time, France decided to support the Mexican conservatives and helped to create a monarchy with archduke Maximilian Habsburg as an emperor of Mexico. However, the liberal leader Benito Juárez never stopped the struggle against French troops and was determined to restore independence and his presidency. He reached this goal in 1867 when French troops were removed from Mexico and Maximilian was captured and executed. The period called 'the second independence' began in Mexico[127]. The liberal reforms in the economic and social sphere, unfortunately did not change the situation of the most marginalized groups, namely the peasantry and urban lower class. Meanwhile, since the 1870s a slow but systematic development of industry appeared in Mexico. After one of the liberal military leaders – Porfirio Díaz took power, it became obvious that only slight changes will take place in the political sphere. He established a longtime dictatorship that was founded on repressions of political enemies and privileges for foreign investors. This situation created favorable conditions for the development of radical ideas. One of the first and most significant was anarchism.

As the first decades of Mexican independence were dominated – in the ideological dimension – by the firm conflict between the liberals and conservatives, there was no space for other ideologies. However, the victory of liberals demonstrated that the successful rejection of conservatism is possible. In reality, taking power by

---

[127] K. Der wich, *W krainie pierzastego węża. Historia Meksyku od podboju do czasów współczesnych*, Cracow, Universitas, 2014, pp. 89-101.

liberals did not change the situation in a significant manner. Specifically, it did not change the situation of the most marginalized masses. The Díaz regime concentrated on the centralization of power. The sphere of civil rights and liberties was very much restricted. However, even before Díaz took power it seemed that Mexican liberals lost their ideals in favor of a sharp struggle for power. That facilitated the spreading of radical ideas that questioned the role of the state and rejected the hitherto order. This favorable atmosphere for radical ideas was also strengthened by the adopted model of economic development. Mexico was opened to foreign capital, mainly north American. It marginalized Mexican society from the benefits of economic development. For the first decades of the 19th-century liberals were perceived as a potential alternative for conservative elites. In the 1870s and 1880s, it appeared that they were, in fact, not interested in a real change of the situation of the poorest sectors of the Mexican society. The conservative elites were not really interested in social and political reforms, therefore it was just a matter of time before any new intellectual alternatives toward conservatism would appear. However, in the mid-19th century, there was no strong tradition of the socialist movement in Mexico, especially in its radical version.

The first attempts of popularizing ideas that rejected the previous order in both the conservative and liberal version appeared in Mexico, as in Argentina and other Latin American countries, thanks to European immigrants. In the case of Mexico, it was Plotino Rhodakanaty. This Greek came to Mexico at the beginning of the 1860s after several years of traveling in Europe. He initiated his activity on Mexican soil as a teacher at a preparatory school (*Escuela Preparatoria*) but quickly lost his post because of his firm critique of Mexican emperor, Maximilian. He then initiated his own Modern and Free School (*Escuela Moderna y Libre*)[128]. As the time went by, Rhodakanaty emerged as the first strong critic of positivist ideas in Mexico, and from 1860-1880 he was probably the most important one. He publicly criticized symbols of Mexican liberalism, as for example the Lerdo Act (*Ley Lerdo*). He appealed to the social revolution that would change the living conditions of the Mexican people. To work with its ideas, he created an organization called *La Social*. It was the first organization in Mexico that was of a pure anarchist nature. In the activity of Plotino Rhodakanaty, one can already observe a significant distinction between the development of Mexican anarchism and the European one. He was convinced that the revolution in Mexico can be carried out in the countryside. Although he lived and worked in Mexico City, he strongly believed that the Mexican peasantry would play a crucial role in the revolution. This assumption was fully reasonable. Mexican peasants were a significant part of the society. This was because of its numbers but also it was the most deprived group. Secondly, differently to Europe, the industrial sector was not yet developed in Mexico. Mexico was a poor agricultural country. If the revolution had to be carried out by the masses, peasants were the only masses. He was critical toward the violent revolutions that were proposed by communists or supporters of Michael Bakunin, however, he accepted the right to rebellion against tyranny. This deep reserve toward violence was visible in the work of Rhodakanaty. He was convinced that teaching and explaining the necessity of radical change is a key factor that can lead to the revolution. That is why he organized his own school. He also created *La Social* for this reason. He had a strong faith that

---

[128] M. Nettlau, *Actividad anarquista en México. Rhodakanaty y Zalacosta. Ricardo Flores Magón, Regeneración y las insurrecciones por 'tierra y libertad'. Apuntes sobre la propaganda anarquista y sindical tardía*, Mexico City, Federal District, Instituto Nacional de Antropología e Historia, 2008.

it is possible to create a just society that can live in harmony[129]. One can find a lot of political thought of Proudhon and Fourier in the ideas of Rhodakanaty. However philosophy of Spinoza, one of the founding fathers of German idealism was the base of Rhodakanaty's thought. Rhodakanaty knew Spinoza's conception of *"Deus sive natura"* well and he constructed his own idea of Christian religion as superior to the others on this foundation. According to him, the foundation of Christianity should be incorporated into social life. Such values as love and harmony are the foundation of this religion and should be the basis on which a socialist society would be created[130]. This particular attitude toward Christianity was something original for Rhodakanaty that distinguished his thought from the socialist and anarchist ideas of European political philosophers. He advocated the idea of peasants and workers community mixed with the Proudhonian criticism of private property and a State. According to him, private poverty is the source of all evil and the biggest enemy of human beings. Basing on the Proudhon's thought, he strongly criticized the institution of a state. For him, state authorities are an instrument of slavery of citizens and create a deep inequality among them. He advocated that there would be no states and governments in a new socialist world. Like Bakunin, he insisted that the idea of real socialism would be born from the class struggle, the struggle between the oppressed and the oppressing. This is an example of the progressive evolution of his ideas from mainly quite moderate and reformist Fourierist thought toward more revolutionary ones, even including an acceptance for the idea of the violent revolution[131]. In his political thought, Rhodakanaty became visibly nearer to some elements of Michael Bakunin's thought. In consequence, taking his

---

[129] C. Illades, *Rhodakanaty y la formación del pensamiento socialista en México*, "Revista Europea de Estudios Latinoamericanos y del Caribe" IX 2004, No. 77, p. 131.

[130] A. J. Cappelletti, *Prologo...*, p. CLXXIX.

[131] *Ibidem*, pp. CLXXX-CLXXXI.

social ideas into account, he can be described as a libertarian socialist or anarcho – syndicalist. He was convinced that his political thought is a strict continuity of the French Revolution and its ideals. He admitted that "the idea of today's socialism is the idea of the French revolution of 1793: Liberty, Equality, and Fraternity, accompanied by Unity"[132]. As radical ideas can be perceived as a kind of development of stronger criticism of conservatism that is proposed by liberals. Rhodakanaty was very critical toward liberalism. He accused liberal leaders of abandoning liberal ideas of freedom, democracy and equality. Instead of that, according to him, liberals created a system based on the exploitation of the masses, that favoring big landlords and capitalists, including foreigners. He remained faithful to the principles of liberal values, that included – among others – federalism and democracy. He talked about going beyond the present civilization which was based, according to him, on a lack of liberty, on poverty, ignorance, and exploitation of the masses through the owners of the capital[133].

As Plotino Rhodakanaty was one of the very first promoters of radical ideas based on anarchist ideology, he also was one of the first initiators of anarchist periodics and organizations. He founded the Students Socialist Group (*Grupo estudiantil socialista*) in 1863. A short time later he initiated the activity of the above mentioned *La Social*. During his activity at this organization, his ideas attracted several students, including: Francisco Zalacosta, Juan Villareal, Hermenegildo Villavicencio and Julio Chávez. They were the first active anarchists in Mexico implementing their ideas into practice. At the beginning of 1870s Juan Villareal founded several workers' organizations. The most important one was The Great Circle of Workers

---

[132] P. C. Rhodakanaty, *Programa social-último sacrificio. Dererminación del nivel histórico*, "El Socialista" V 1876, No. 178, cit., *ibidem*, p. CLXXIX.

[133] C. Illades, *Rhodakanaty y la formación del pensamiento socialista en México*, Rubí, Barcelona, Anthropos Editorial, 2002, p. 58.

of Mexico (*El Gran Circulo de Obreros de México*)[134]. Together with *La Social*, it was the first workers' organization in Mexico. However, because of the weakness of the industrial sector and the labor class, both Rhodakanaty and some of its followers were convinced that the only way to create a socialist society is a peasant revolution accompanied by the crawling industrial sector and its workers. It seems that the most important promoter of this idea was Julio Chávez. He was the head of the most important peasant insurgency movement in the end of 19th century. He initiated a process of expropriating of the lands in the Chalco – Texcoco region. The process quickly expanded. Chávez described himself as an anarcho-communist as he was against any form of government and wanted collective lands[135]. In his manifesto published in January 1868 and titled *Republic and Homeland Mexico*, he called on President Benito Juárez to implement a land reform. He wrote: "No one is born to serve the other, every one who can use his mind and is not contaminated by bad habits, has the right to designate who would guide common interests of all people"[136]. In another manifesto – *To All Oppressed and Poor of Mexico and the World* – Chávez presented his fully anarchist ideas: "The hour has come for all people of a good heart to know; the day has come in which the enslaved would rise up as man demanding their rights demolished by those who have power. (…) Brothers, the moment has come to clear up the countryside, to compensate the bills by those who always requested us to pay them; this is the

---

[134] M. Nettlau, *op. cit.*, p. 27.

[135] A. J. Cappelletti, *Prologo…*, p. CLXXXI.

[136] "(…) nadie nació para servir a otro, todo el que tiene espedito el uso de su razón y no se ha contaminado con los vicios, tiene derecho a designar a quienes han de cuidar de los intereses comunes a todos los hobres (…)", cit. in: D. Carmona, *Es fusilado Julio López, calificado de "comunista, asesino y gavillero"*, "Memoria Política de México" 9 VII 1868, www.memoriapoliticademexico.org/Efemerides/7/09071868-JCh.html (31.01.2015).

day of imposing the duties to all those who wants rights only. Those who were taking advantage of our physical, moral and intellectual weakness they are landlords and *hacendados*. (…) We want to reject all that marks tyranny between people, we want to live at societies in fraternity, mutualism and to establish the Universal Republic of Harmony"[137].

The activity of Rhodakanaty and its collaborators and successors was the first organized effort to initiate a revolution that would implement anarchist ideals on Mexican soil. He was not the only one who believed that the revolution leading to the establishment of the ideal socialist society should begin in the countryside. José Maria González was another anarchist leader who led a peasant rebellion. Inspired by Proudhon, Bakunin and also by Mexican anarchist Francisco Zuluaga, he took up arms in 1877. After its defeat a few years later, several other peasant rebellions took place. They were of a local nature and none of them were of crucial importance.

During the liberal governments of Benito Juárez and Sebastian Lerdo de Tejada, anarchists and radical activists had a broad range of freedom in their activity, provided they did not take any illegal steps, as for example Chávez, in his attempt to expropriate private property. The situation changed significantly during the regime of Porfirio Díaz. The dictatorship based on repressions and huge restrictions in the area of civil liberties, resulted in difficult times

---

[137] "Ha llegado la hora de conocer a los hombres con el corazón bien puesto; ha llegado el día en que los esclavos se levanten cono un solo hombre reclamado sus derechos pisoteados por los poderosos (…) Hermanos: ha llegado el momento de despejar el campo, de pedir cuentas a lso que siempre nos las han exigido; es el día de imponer deberes a quienes sólo han querido derechos. Los que se han aprovechado de nuestra debilidad física, moral e intelectual se llaman latifundistas, terratenientes o hacendados. Los que pacientements nos llamamos trabajadores, proletarios o peones. (…) Queremos abolir todo lo que sea señal de tirranía entre los mismos hombres, viviendo en sociedades de fraternidad y mutualismo e estableciendo la República Universal de la Armonía", source: *ibidem*.

for all critics of Porfirio and his rule. Most of them were put into jail or were subjected to other forms of repression. Simultaneously, Díaz adopted the model of economic development that strongly supported foreign investors, both in agriculture and industry, that heavily exploited the Mexican labor force. Rapid economic growth did not mean better living conditions for the Mexican society. However, in Mexico, an unprecedented development of railways could be observed. The Porfirian era was also a period of intensive industrialization process. Foreign companies invested huge capital in the oil, mining, textile industry and other sectors. There was a also huge concentration of land in hands of great landowners, in large part foreigners during the Porfirian era. The significant development of the industrial sector also led to the appearance of numbers of workers, nevertheless, Mexico still was a rural country. A grand majority of the Mexican society lived in the countryside and over 60% of the labor force in Mexico worked in agriculture[138]. Changes that took place in Mexico during the Porfirian era also created new conditions for the development of radical ideas. A growing number of workers and the slow but visible growth of the urban population gave an impulse to take more active efforts to mobilize also these groups of the Mexican society in the struggle for the revolution that would change social conditions in the country. That explains why anarchist leaders focused more attention toward workers and the urban population. Both Rhodakanaty and his collaborators were well aware of this situation. They reorganized *La Social* to disseminate their ideas among the workers of Mexico City. Zalacosta was especially convinced that it is possible to incite a revolution that would destroy the previous order built on the capitalist exploitation of the labor masses. He was strongly engaged in publishing propagandist

---

[138] J. G o d i o, *Historia del movimiento obrero latinoamericano*, Vol. 1, Mexico, Nueva Sociedad, 1983, p. 268.

periodics. One of them was *La Internacional*. On the pages of one of the issues of this weekly magazine in 1876, Zalacosta wrote: "Our programme: social anarchy, abolishing all governments and social revolution"[139]. Also, The Great Circle of Workers of Mexico was quite active during the entire decade of the 1870s. In this period, the organization undertook direct acts of disobedience and initiated its struggle against capitalists. The most popular form were strikes, primarily in the Federal District. Also, the Great Circle of Workers of Mexico organized the Worker's Congress organizations. However, with the growth of repressions after taking power by Porfirio Díaz, the majority of anarchist leaders was arrested or had to disappear from the public. In effect, Zalacosta was arrested in 1880 and was executed by the Mexican army. Meanwhile, Rhodakanty was active in the conspiracy for some time. He left Mexico City to teach in Ajusco, where he taught numerous students. His writings gave purpose and direction to the labor movement until 1880. After several years, in 1886, Plotino Rhodakanaty returned to Europe. It is interesting that after his departure, no additional information was known about him. As a result of his disappearance during the 1880s, there was a significant crisis in the activity of any anarchist movements in Mexico.

A new wave of anarchist ideas emerged in Mexico at the turn of the 19th and 20th century. Again, it can be perceived as a kind of natural evolution from liberal opposition toward conservative values. However, it seems that the most important factor that stimulated – both limited and radical – opposition was the Porfirista regime. Its indolence to resolve conflicts with the developing labor movement led to significant tensions. In effect, more or less important workers organizations have been functioning in Mexico since the beginning

---

[139] "Nuestro programa: la anarquía social, la abolición de todos los gobiernos y la revolución social", M. Nettlau, *op. cit.*, p. 30.

of the Porfirio regime. For several years, their demands were limited to social postulates: 8-hour working day, insurance, salary increase etc. The expression of workers' struggle for better working conditions was a growing number of strikes. During the entire Porfirian era, between 1876-1911, about 250 strikes were registered[140]. This was a significant number for a country where the industrialization process had just began. Much more ideological diversity could be observed among the organizations as they included: anarchists, syndicalists, and socialists, to mention the most important ones. This struggle between Mexican workers for better social conditions was accompanied by growing disappointment as a result of Díaz's long regime based on the rule of a strictly limited group of so-called *scientificos* and police. At the beginning of the 20th century, a new kind of opposition emerged in the form of the Mexican Liberal Party. Its leader was Ricardo Flores Magón, a man that in a short time became the real father of Mexican anarchism. As Benito Juárez is still the symbol of Mexican liberalism today, Ricardo Flores Magón remains the symbol of anarchist ideas in Mexico. However, it seems justified to agree with a brilliant Mexican thinker and philosopher Lepoldo Zea that Ricardo Magón was strongly inspired by positivist thought. As it was presented in the earlier chapter, positivist ideas that came from Europe to Latin American countries became very popular, although they were transformed to particular realities of those countries. The same can be said about anarchist thought in Mexico[141]. As some ideas of Mexican positivists and anarchists were quite similar, there is no doubt that the latter were much more radical in their views and demands. They were much more militant in their activity,

---

[140] C. A. Ribera, *La Casa del Obrero Mundial. Anarcosindicalismo y revolución en México*, Mexico City, Federal District, Instituto Nacional de Antropología e Historia, 2010, p. 29.

[141] L. Zea, *Del liberalismo a la revolución en la educación mexicana*, Mexico City, Talleres Gráficos de la Nación, 1956, p. 93.

too. It is worth remembering that the roots of Ricardo Magón's ideas originated in positivism and evolved from liberal ones to much more radical and finally took on the form of pure anarchism. However, this was anarchism with particular Mexican characteristics. A slow divorce of Ricardo Magón and positivist ideas can be observed since the moment he quit his education at the university. In 1892, he experienced his first imprisonment as he was arrested for the first time by the regime of Porfirio Díaz[142]. It was the first step toward the radicalization of his attitude toward the reality that he was surrounded by. It was the exemplification of growing activity of the new generation. At the turn of the 19th and 20th centuries, such important thinkers as: José Vasconselos, Bernardo Reyes, Antonio Caso or Francisco I. Madero began their public activity. Undoubtedly, Ricardo Flores Magón became the most radical one among them.

It is not an easy task to precisely define anarchist ideology as it has various forms and currents, it is necessary to point out some basic postulates presented by the leaders of anarchist movements in Mexico. First of all, anarchist ideas were born from the deep preoccupation of social conditions that were a daily reality for a huge part of the Mexican society. According to this, the resolution of this difficult situation can be only the total resignation from private property and establishing collective property. This could drive people toward happiness and prosperity. Anarchists were strongly skeptic about the institution of a state that was perceived as a source of repression[143]. Those general assumptions were accompanied by various peculiarities that were added by different thinkers, as: Bakunin, Kropotkin, Proudhon, Fourier etc. One can ask about the lack of Karl Marx among those who inspired Ricardo Flores Magón and

---

[142] M. Nettlau, *op. cit.*, p. 34.
[143] E. Blanquel, J. MacGregor, *Ricardo Flores Magón y la revolución mexicana, y otros ensayos históricos*, Mexico City, Federal District, El Colegio de México, 2008, p. 67.

other anarchists in Mexico. This is quite easy to explain. First of all, there was a fundamental difference in the goals of Marxist social-ism and anarchism. The first one desired to establish some kind of proletarian dictatorship. For anarchists there was no difference in any dictatorships – neither personal, as it was in the case of Porfirio Diaz in Mexico – nor other ones. Also, Marxist ideas were not par-ticularly popular in Mexico. It is worth emphasizing that there was much more support and favor to various forms of anarchism than to socialism in the form proposed by Karl Marx. What is character-istic for anarchist thought in Mexico, and *magónismo*, in particular, is the evident evolution of it from the liberal ideas. As one takes the process of liberalism's development as a kind of continuum, the anarchist thought should be perceived as the last, the most radical phase of it. It can be observed pretty well in the attitude toward the institution of a state. In liberal thought, one can observe vari-ous beliefs on how limited a state should be. Anarchism goes much further – for anarchists it does not matter what form it adopts as they reject the institution of the state in general. For them, it was not important what the government is allowed to do because they believe that the best government is which does not exist. It can be concluded that in the political sense, anarchism is a form of radical liberalism that is strongly similar to libertarian thought. However, there is a significant difference between anarchism and libertarian-ism in the area of the economy. In this sphere, anarchism adopts some socialist ideas with the fundamental one which is the abolition of private property[144].

All of these general remarks about anarchism are important in the case of the presentation of Ricardo Flores Magón's thought. His public activity also demonstrates the evolution of *magónismo* very well. Since he started as a liberal that had strongly criticized the

---

[144] *Ibidem*, pp. 78-79.

Porfiriat system, his later writings include radical anarchist ideas. As it was mentioned above, Ricardo Flores Magón was engaged in different anti-Porfirista initiatives since the last decade of the 19th century. Meanwhile, clubs where different political and economic ideas were discussed were already appearing in Mexico at the beginning of the 1900s. Already in 1900, Camilo Ariaga organized the founding meeting of the Liberal Party. In a short time, liberal clubs across the country appeared, primarily in the north and the majority in the capital. At the beginning, the uniting factor was the objection to Diaz's overly conciliatory attitude toward the Catholic Church. The Flores Magón brothers – Ricardo, Jesús, Enrique – and Antonio Díaz Soto y Gama, among others, initiated their political careers in those clubs. The *Regeneración* periodical, where Ricardo Flores Magón published a lot of its articles, became their most important instrument of propaganda. The publishing of periodicals was the most important and effective instrument of the popularization of their ideas. Although Ricardo was repressed in Mexico and after going to the United States spent a long time in US prisons, after being released he always returned to the publishing his *Regeneración*. However, the ideological differences caused the division in the movement. The Flores Magón brothers had already come into contact with anarchist leaders, such as, for example Emma Goldman or Florencio Bazorra. This also had a significant impact on the radicalization of Ricardo's ideas[145].

On the base of the group engaged in publishing *Regeneración*, Ricardo decided to found a political organization which took the shape of Mexican Liberal Party (*Partido Liberal Mexicano* – PLM). Its founding fathers included close collaborators of Ricardo Flores Magón: Juan Sarabia, Antonio I. Villareal and Librado Rivera. The principal aim of the party was to struggle with the Díaz regime using

---

[145] K. Derwich, *op. cit.*, p. 117.

all possible instruments. Since the very beginning, Ricardo and the PLM cooperated closely with various radical leaders from the United States. As Ricardo was the most important ideologist of the party, a closer analysis of the PLM program would also demonstrate a general picture of Flores Magón's ideas. A very strong demand to respect full freedom of speech and press could be found. As it was characteristic for all anarchists, the party also required a complete resignation from obligatory military service. According to the PLM, it was the worst form of oppression and was completely in opposition to the rights of every citizen. They also condemned military courts and wanted to judge soldiers accused of criminal acts by civil courts[146]. A lot of space in the document was dedicated to the Catholic Church. It was emphasized that the clergy undertake activities strongly exceeding their religious mission. There is a strong condemnation of the political engagement of the Catholic hierarchy in the politics and the accusation of being a significant obstacle on the way toward democratic institutions. The catholic clergy was accused of engagement in economic activity as well, which led, according to the PLM, to the exploitation of Mexican society and its impoverishment[147]. As all liberals, the PLM and their leaders that also had much more radical views, strongly criticized the educational system which was dominated by the clergy. "The liquidation of the clergy schools would end the focal point of divisions and hatred between the sons of Mexico, it would lay foundations for the full fraternity of the great Mexican family in the future"[148]. As most of the founding fathers of the PLM were much more radical than the traditional liberal leaders,

---

[146] *Programa del Partido Liberal y Manifesto a la Nación*, 1 de Julio 1906 [in:] C. M. Rama, A. J. Cappelletti, *op. cit.*, p. 357.

[147] *Ibidem*, pp. 358-359.

[148] "Suprimir la escuela clrerical es Anabar con el foco de las divisiones y los odios entre los hijos de México, es cimentar sobre la más sólida base, para futuro próximo, la completa fraternidad de la gran familia mexicana", *ibidem*, p. 360.

they could not miss the social elements in the program of the party. A strong critique of the Díaz regime can be found, not only by the prism of its dictatorial nature but also as a regime that was totally unable to resolve the problems of the labor masses, that is workers and peasants. In effect, the PLM perceived the eight hour day and increase of salaries to the level of one peso per hour as a minimum condition. The improvement of working conditions in the sense of hygiene was of particular importance. Finally, the typical demands raised by the PLM were the prohibition of child labor, salaries paid in cash and compensation for accidents etc. Angél Cappelletti made an accurate observation that the program of the PLM was a kind of predecessor of the Mexican Revolution. It articulated all postulates that later would have been included to the Constitution of 1917[149]. For example, their program stated that *ejidos* which was a traditional collective form of land property among indigenous communities should be restored[150]. This is exactly the same claim that will raised ten years later by Emiliano Zapata.

There is no doubt that PLM program was an effect of a fragile compromise. Firstly, the already anarchist views of Ricardo Flores Magón were strictly limited. However, the PLM program was much more radical than the traditional liberal postulates.

As time went by, the radicalization of Ricardo Flores Magón also influenced the PLM. This was perfectly visible after the eruption of the Mexican Revolution. For him, the overthrow of Profirio Díaz was just a first step toward a real revolution. It was a *sine qua non* condition to start the process of building a more just society. Meanwhile, the interim government of Francisco León de la Barra was, according to Flores Magón, the new incarnation of the old regime. Also, the godfather of the Mexican revolution – Francisco I. Madero

---

[149] A. J. Cappelletti, *Prologo...*, p. CLXXXVI.
[150] "La restitución de ejidos a los pueblos que han sido despojados de ellos es de clara justicia", *Programa del Partido Liberal...*, p. 364.

– did not guarantee a real revolution and the abolishment of the old order. This radicalization is perfectly visible in the PLM's Manifest dated September 23, 1911, ten months after the revolution began. One can easily find statements that sound like a typical anarchist manifesto.

> To abolish this principle (private property – M. M, K. D.) means annihilation of all political, economic, social, religious and moral institutions that comprise the environment in which the free initiative and free association of human beings is strangled and they are obliged – to not die – but to initiate a fierce competence between them, which is won not by the best ones, not by the most selfless, not by the most physically, morally or intellectually talented, but the most clever, egoist, those without scruples (…).
>
> Without the principle of private property no government has a reason to exist (…) the Church also has no reason to exist, because it's only aim is to supress inherent rebellion against the oppression and exploitation of mankind (…) Capital, Authority, Clergy: this is the somber trinity (…)[151].

The elimination of the private property for Flores Magón and other anarchist leaders in Mexico was of fundamental meaning. It was not only a preferred form of property but also, it was a key to change the system in other dimensions. For example, he perceived it as a mean to construct a really democratic society. Eduardo

---

[151] "Abolir ese principio significa el aniquilamiento de todas las instituciones políticas, económicas, sociales, religiosas y morales que componen el ambiente dentro del cual se asfixian la libre iniciativa y la libre asosciación de los seres humanos que se ven obligados, para no perecer, a entablar entre si una encarnizada competencia, de la que salen triunfantes, no los más buenos, no los más abnegados, no los mejor dotados en lo físico, en lo moral o en los intelectual, sino los más astutos, los más egoístas, los menos esxruptulosos (…). Sin el principio de la propiedad privada no tiene razón el Gobierno (…) ni tendrá razón de ser la Iglesia, cuyo exclusivo objetivo es estrangular e el ser humano la innata rebeldía contra la opresión y la explotación (…) Capital, Autoridad, Clero: he ahí la trinidad sombría (…)". *Manifesto del Partido Liberal Mexicano*, September 23, 1911, [in:] C. M. Rama, A. J. Cappelletti, *op. cit.*, p. 376.

Balanquel cites an interesting quote of Ricardo Flores Magón: "The masses took the divine institution in their hands... (it was already forgotten that it was God himself who governed by the king?)..., they destroyed it and governed themselves remove privileges and to obtain freedom, justice and wealth for all, but- making everyone free and happy [failed] (…) this is due to the fact that the source where all privileges and inequality came from was left intact; namely private property"[152].

In his desire to destroy private property and to abolish a state and government Ricardo Flores Magón displayed himself as an authentic revolutionary anarchist. Returning to the Manifest dated September 1911, he expressed what he believed for many years, the division of classes and the conflict between them. According to him, society was divided between the capitalists and those who work – workers and peasants. As they represented completely different spheres, the conflict was permanent and inevitable. In the Manifest one could read: "(…) two social classes of completely contrary interests: the class of capitalists and the working class; the class that posses the land, means of production and the means of transportation of wealth and the class that cannot count on anything apart from their arms and intelligence to provide them food. No friendship or fraternity can exist between these two social classes because the class of the owners is always ready to perpetuate the economic, political and social system which guarantees a calm enjoyment of their robberies, meanwhile, the working class carries out efforts to destroy

---

[152] "Las masas tomaron en sus manos la institución divina (…) (se ha olvidado ya que fue el mismo Dios el que goebrnó por medio del rey?) (…), la destruyeron y trataron de gobernarse a sí mismos para suprimir el privilegio y obtener la libertad, la justicia y el bienestar para todos, [pero su fracaso en] hacer a todos libres y felices (…) se debió al hecho de que dejó intacta la fuente de dodned provenía el privilegio y la desigualdad; esto es, la propiedad privada", cit. in: E. Blanquel, J. MacGregor, op. cit., p. 86.

this unfair system to establish one in which lands, houses, means of production and transportation would be of common use"[153].

It is worth remembering that the beginning of the Mexican revolution permitted various ideas to be presented and alternatives to create a new political, economic and social reality in Mexico. Therefore, Mexican revolution from the very beginning was multidimensional. There was a Madero current that can be perceived as traditional liberalism, well known in Mexico. However, there was also a much more radical face of the revolution which was Emiliano Zapata. His slogan Land and Liberty (¡Tierra y Libertad!) was in fact nothing new. It was one of the postulates already expressed by Ricardo Flores Magón and the PLM. Since the very beginning of the revolution, the Magón brothers and their collaborators were pretty active. What was the goal for one group, was just a first step for Ricardo. His aim was to establish a real social and economic emancipation of the working class. He desired to give the lands and means of production to those who produce. For him, any government was a representative of the capitalists. That is why he perceived the introduction of his postulates and the PLM's program by the political means as impossible. Ricardo Flores Magón did not have any doubts that the revolution led by Francisco I. Madero was a bourgeoisie revolution. Meanwhile, he wanted a revolution that would destroy the old regime not only in the form of the Porfirian regime but in

---

[153] "(…) dos clases sociales de interesem diametralmente opuestos: la clase kapitalista y la clase trabajadora; la clase que posee la tierra, la maquinaria de producción y los medios de transportación de las riquezas, y la clase que no cuenta más que con sus brazos y su inteligencia para proporcionarse es sustento. Entre estas dos clases sociales no puede existir vínculo de amistad y fraternidad, porque la claes poseedora está siempre dispuesta a perpetuar el sistema económico, político y social que garantiza el tranquilo disfrute de sus rapiñas, mientras la clase trabajadora hace esfuerzo por destruir ese sistema inicuo para instaurar un medio en el cual la tierra, las casas, la maquinaria de producción y los medios de transportación sean de uso común", ibidem, pp. 376-377.

every possible dimension. In his views, a lot could be observed from Kropotkin ideas.

What is particularly important, not only in *magónismo* but in Mexican anarchist thought, in general, is the great attention paid to the problem of the land. This was already well visible in the first generation of Mexican anarchists, as Rhodakanaty or Chávez, and was still present at the beginning of the 20<sup>th</sup> century. Meanwhile, the land reform became one of the focal points of the revolution. In June 1914, Ricardo Magón wrote at *Regeneración*, "No, [we] may not resign from the distribution of the lands; one must take it all to make it a common property, not individual one"[154]. As during the Porfirian era in Mexico, there was a significant development of industry, it was natural that anarchists had to pay attention not only to peasants as an exploited group but also toward workers. In his ideas, Flores Magón had the same resolution for any form of private property and expropriation of the working class – a complete abolition of that form. According to him, this is something inconsistent with natural law. "(…) take the land, but not for your own, for you and for all, because it belongs to everyone according to natural law"[155]. In 1910, he wrote: "The land that due to natural law cannot be accumulated by a few but constitutes the property of all human beings"[156]. He argued, that the common form of property already existed in Mexico and was brutally interrupted by the Spanish conquest. In fact, the traditional *ejidos* was a form of common property among some in-

---

[154] "No, no hay que conformarse con los repartos de tierra; hay que tomarlo todo para hacerlo propiedad común (…)", cit. in: A. J. Cappelletti, *Prologo…*, pp. CXCVII-CXCVIII.

[155] "(…) toma la tierra, pero no para ti solo, para ti y para todos los demás, pues que de todos es por derecho natural", E. Blanquel, J. MacGregor, *op. cit.*, p. 91.

[156] "(…) posesión de la tierra que, por derecho natural, no puede ser acaparada por unos cuantos, sino que es la propiedad de todo ser humano", R. Flores Magón, *Regeneración*, November 19, 1910, [in:] C. M. Rama, A. J. Cappelletti, *op. cit.*, p. 396.

digenous groups. Restoration of the *ejidos* and redistribution of the land to this communities was also a priority for Emiliano Zapata and his revolutionary struggle. However, the nature of the Magon's and Zapata's struggle was quite different, in the case of *tierra y libertad* they had the same aims.

*Magónismo* appeared to be the most influential exemplification of anarchist ideas in Mexico at the turn of the 19th and 20th century. As it grew out of liberalism and positivism, it emerged to be the most radical thought in Mexico of that time. In distinction with the earlier anarchist ideas proposed by Rhodakanaty and his collaborators, Ricardo Flóres Magón created a coherent program that he wanted to introduce. What needs a strong emphasis, he did not exclude the possibility of implementing its goals by means of a political competition. Although he perceived rebellion as a natural right that is entitled to all people[157] – another connotation with classical liberalism derived from John Locke, among others, (just to mention the Declaration of Independence of the United States[158]) – he decided to establish and develop the PLM. It was for a long time a principal anarchist organization in Mexico. This is very particular for Mexican anarchism. In general, anarchists condemned creating political parties because they were perceived by them as an instru-

---

[157] "Supremo derecho de los instantes supremos es la rebeldía. Sin ella, la humanidad andaría perdida aún en aquel lejano crepúsculo que la historia llama la edad de la piedra; sin ella la inteligencia humana hace tiempo que habría naufragado en el lodo de los dogmas (…)", R. Flores Magón, *Regeneración*, September 10, 1910, [in:] C. M. Rama, A. J. Cappelletti, *op. cit.*, p. 387.

[158] The Declaration of Independence says: "(…) whenever any Form of Government becomes destructive of these ends, it is the Right of the People to alter or to abolish it, and to institute new Government, laying its foundation on such principles and organizing its powers in such form, as to them shall seem most likely to affect their Safety and Happiness (…)", *Declaration of Independence*, July 4, 1776, [in:] R. Kłosowicz, *Documents and Readings in American History: From the Colonies to the End of the Nineteenth Century*, Cracow, WUJ, 2005, p. 56.

ment of the capitalist system. Abolition of a state and government for the great majority of anarchists also meant the condemnation of political parties as a part of the hated system. If they decided to organize themselves, it was principally syndicates. The workers was the basic group that – according to anarchists – should initiate a revolution for a better working conditions and the creation of a new, more just and proper order. That was the way the anarchist organizations were acting, for example, in Argentina. FORA was the most important anarchist organization not only in Argentina but in South America in general. In Mexico, the first syndicates were created at the beginning of the 20th century. The Confederation of Printers (*Confederación de Tipógrafos*) was one of the very first. The organization of anarcho – syndicalism in Mexico was the effect of Juan Francisco Moncaleano coming to this country. He was a Colombian activist that came to Mexico in 1912. Together with some Mexicans, he created *Grupo Anarquista Luz*. In the Manifest of the group, Moncaleano wrote: "(…) to rebel against the oppression of humanity's persecutors: clergy, government, and capital. (…) [to – K. D.] proclaim that we all are equal because we all are governed by the same natural laws and not by the fanciful ones. (…) our goal is to achieve freedom for enslaved workers. Our weapon is truth against injustice. (…) We march forward toward the ideal redeemer, toward the universal homeland where we all could live in mutual respect and absolute freedom; without fathers of the homeland, without gods of heavens and insolent rich men"[159].

---

[159] "(…) Rebelarse al yugo de los verdugos de la humanidad: clero, gobierno y capital. (…) Pregonar que todos somos iguales porque todos estamos regidos por los mismos efectos de las leyes naturales y no por leyes caprichosas. (…) Nuestro fin es conseguir la libertad del obrero esclavizado. Nuestra arma es la verdad contra la iniquidad. (…) Marchamos adelante hacia el ideal redentor, hacia la patria universal donde todos podamos vivir dentro del respeto mutuo en absoluta libertad; sin padres de la patria,

Together with representatives of other workers organizations the members of the *Grupo Anarquista Luz* met together in Mexico City in September 1912 to establish the most important workers anarcho – syndicalist organization during the Mexican Revolution – the House of Workers (*La Casa de Obrero*). However, it disappeared when the Regional Confederation of Mexican Workers (*Confederación Regional de Obreros de México* – CROM) was created in 1918.

The Mexican Revolution was also a factor that strongly influenced development and radicalization of Ricardo Flores Magón anarchists views. The revolution created favorable conditions for the struggle with the odious system. It not only overthrew the Porfirio Díaz regime but also focused on themes that were previously practically absent in the public discourse. The revolution gave a possibility to present their ideas to all groups. *Magónismo* – based on the anarchist thought – was just one among many. As this was probably the most radical one, it was not easy to promote it freely. Ricardo strongly cooperated with US anarchists, which resulted in several arrests and years spent in US prisons. In fact, his struggle for the new order became limited to publishing activities, mostly in his *Regeneración*, periodical where he always published when he was not in prison. However, he was not alone. *Magónismo* had a well organized net of supporters and Flores Magón cooperated with other anarchists in Mexico. The PLM's founding fathers were the core group. It is necessary to mention Práxedis Guerrero, among others. Although he was not in the group of the closest collaborators of Ricardo Flores Magón and the PLM, he was an active intellectual supporting anarchist ideas of Magón and enriching Mexican anarchist thought. He wrote several articles that were published in *Regeneración*. Práxedis Guerrero also based his ideas on the division of society into two

---

sin dioses de los cielos ni ricos insolentes", *Manifiesto Anarquista del Grupo Luz*, [in:] C. A. Ribera, *op. cit.*, p. 40.

classes. "The heritage, education, dissimilarity in living conditions created significant differences, both moral and physical, between the bourgeoisie and proletarians (…)"[160]. As it can be observed, this division was the foundation of the previous order. To change the order, it was necessary, according to anarchists, to abolish the capitalist class, the owners of the lands, of means of production and the means of transportation.

The anarchist movement did not reach its goals in Mexico. However, there is no doubt that there are very few countries where the influence of anarchist ideas was so commonly known and had such a large impact on changing the reality. As the beginnings of anarchist thought in Mexico were quite difficult – first, the French intervention and the restoration of independence and later the Porfirio Díaz regime, it was permanently present. Since the time Rhodakanaty planted the seed of anarchist ideas on the Mexican soil, this radical thought has never disappeared. The *magónismo* was the most developed and the most complete version of Mexican anarchist thought which was not just a European import. Mexican reality extorted some changes in it. It is another example, after positivism, which confirms the thesis that there are strong arguments in favor of the conclusion that Latin American thought already existed at the turn of the 19th and 20th century.

---

[160] "La herencia, la educación, la desemejanza de las circunstancias de vida, habrán creado diferencias profundas, morales y hasta físicas entre burgeses y proletarios (…)", P. Guerrer, *Regeneración*, September 10, 1910, [in:] C. M. Rama, A. J. Cappelletti, *op. cit.*, pp. 419-420.

DOI: 10.12797/9788376386775.05

# INSTEAD OF CONCLUSION

Several observations can be formulated as a result of his brief research dedicated to the subject of Latin American thought:

- there is a great need to research and analyze all that constitutes
  Latin American thought;
- it is of great importance to research the methods and paradigms
  related to Latin American thought;
- there is a fundamental debate related to the question whether
  Latin American thought exists and the conclusion is that this debate is not yet settled;
- there is a broad tradition of Latin American "pensamiento".

Regarding the first observation, Latin America constitutes a
very important subject of contemporary academic analysis. It is the
subject of different academic disciplines, from archeology, history,
through geography, anthropology, political science, to the humanities in a broad sense. The importance of a broad reflection on Latin
America can be observed during various international congresses
dedicated to the topic of Latin American. The International Congresses of Americanists, which are a great opportunity for all aca-
demics dedicated to researching Latin America to exchange the effects of their explorations is worth mentioning. Researching Latin
American thought is of great importance for Latin American studies
in general. It allows for a better understanding of the distinctiveness

of the region. Also, a broad reflection over the Latin American thought can help in better understanding of the mutual relations between the Latin American and European continent. The impact of the European civilization on the New World cannot be denied. However, the influence, even if it takes a great form does not have to mean a similarity. This is the answer to the question of whether there is any need to research Latin American thought.

In the case of methods and paradigms, a great necessity of further research can also be observed. This is justified by deep distinctions between Latin American tradition and European one. As Europe has its great impact on Latin American development in almost every sense, it is still just one of the foundations that constitute contemporary Latin America. The pre-Hispanic heritage cannot be forgotten. However, since the fall of Spanish and Portuguese colonial empires and the beginning of independent states, Latin America began to create its own formula. However, methods and paradigms used in researching Latin American thought still constitute some controversies. The application of particular paradigms can lead to some kind of ballasts in the process of academic reflection. In this study, we have adopted and analyzed four principal paradigms that dominate in the broad reflection on Latin American thought: 1) the question of cultural imperialism, 2) the question of existence and identity, 3) the question of conquest, and 4) the question of modernization. Their closer analysis demonstrates the importance of the consciousness of their existence and their impact on the process of exploring Latin American thought and also the large necessity if researching methods and paradigms in Latin American thought.

The great difficulty of the studies dedicated to Latin American thought is the existing uncertainty if discussing this phenomenon is justified. We do not aspire to give one precise answer to this question. As the two cases analyzed in this book show, uncertainty is an inherent part of the explorations of the Latin American contribution to philosophy. The case of positivism clearly demonstrates that not only the adoption of European philosophical ideas occurred in the Latin American and Caribbean regions but also their further development and adaptation to the particular Latin American conditions. Some European ideas were barely transformed by Latin American intellectuals, which gave them an entirely new nature. It can be perceived as an argument toward the existence of Latin American thought, distinctive from European or North American thought. However, the second case analyzed in this study can be perceived as an opposite reasoning. Although anarchism, especially in Mexico, had its peculiar characteristics, it was brought to Latin America by foreigners (Europeans and North Americans). It was also adopted by Latin American activists and intellectuals without a far-reaching transformation. Compared to positivist thought, anarchist ideas were quite well suited to the Latin American reality at the turn of the 19th and 20th century. As the capitalist system that was developing in the Latin American republics did not differentiate strongly from other regions of the world, the alternatives proposed by Latin American anarchists were quite the same. The difference between positivism and anarchism also results from their range. Positivism was a very broad proposition of formulating all spheres of peoples' lives. It was not based on economic or social division. It was a probe of new order. On the other hand, anarchism was a form of rejection of the previous economic and social order. It can be described as a narrower proposition. However, both cases cannot solve "endless dilemma" of the existence or lack of Latin American thought.

Finally, it has to be accepted that since its independence, Latin America has formulated its own identity, also in the intellectual sphere. As the region has its characteristic in every aspect of its existence, the peculiarity of the Latin American "pensamiento" should be respected. It can only be measured by Latin American measurements. Putting European forms of measurement can be ballasted by

Eurocentric theses and marks. Although it cannot be understood as an argument against European studies on Latin American thought, every kind of reflection can lead to a better understanding of Latin America. It's better understanding also leads to its development and self-determination.

# BIBLIOGRAPHY

Alberdi J. B., *Bases y puntos de partida para la organización política de la Republica Argentina*, [in:] L. Zea, *Pensamiento positivista latinoamericano*, Caracas, Venezuela, Biblioteca Ayacucho, 1980.

Alberdi J. B., *Ideas para presidir a la confección del curso de filosofía contemporánea*, [in:] idem, *Escritos póstumos. Memorias y documentos*, Vol. 15, Buenos Aires, Imprenta europea, 1900.

Alberdi J. B., *Ideas para presidir a la confección del curso de filosofía contemporánea*, [in:] L. Zea, *Pensamiento positivista latinoamericano*, Caracas, Venezuela, Biblioteca Ayacucho, 1980.

Alberdi J. B., *Ideas para presidir a la confección del curso de filosofía contemporánea*, [in:] J. Gaos, *El pensamiento hispanoamericano. Antología del pensamiento de lengua española en la edad contemporánea*, Mexico City, National Autonomous University of Mexico, Coordinación de Humanidades, 1993.

Alberini C., *Contemporary Philosophic Tendencies in South America, With Special Reference to Argentina*, „Monist" 1927, Vol. 37, No. 3.

Alcoff L. M., *Mignolo's Epistemology of Coloniality*, „CR: The New Centennial Review" 2008, Vol. 7, No. 3.

Ardao A., *Assimilation and Transformation of Positivism in Latin America*, „Journal of the History of Ideas" X-XII 1963, Vol. 24, No. 4.

Ardao A., *Historia y evolución de las ideas filosóficas en América Latina*, „Proceedings of the IX Inter-American Congress of Philosophy" 1979, Vol. 1.

Arguedas A., *La dictadura y la anarquia*, [in:] L. Zea, *Pensamiento positivista latinoamericano*, Caracas, Venezuela, Biblioteca Ayacucho, 1980.

Armstrong A. M., *Contemporary Latin-American Philosophy*, „The Philosophical Quarterly" 1953, Vol. 3, No. 11.

Baldwin Th. (ed.), *The Cambridge History of Philosophy 1870-1945*, Cambridge, Cambridge University Press, 2003 [online:] http://dx.doi.org/10.1017/CHOL9780521591041.

Barker C., Galasinski D., *Cultural Studies and Discourse Analysis a Dialogue on Language and Identity*, London, SAGE, 2001.

Barker Ch., *The Sage Dictionary of Cultural Studies*, London, SAGE, 2004.

Beuchot M., *The History of Philosophy in Colonial Mexico*, Washington, D. C., Catholic University of America Press, 1998.

Beuchot M., *The Study of the Philosophy's History in Mexico as a Foundation for Doing Mexican Philosophy*, [in:] A. Salles, E. Millán-Zaibert (eds.), *The Role of History in Latin American Philosophy: Contemporary Perspectives*, Albany, New York, SUNY Press, 2005.

Blanquel E., MacGregor J., *Ricardo Flores Magón y la revolución mexicana, y otros ensayos históricos*, Mexico City, Federal District, El Colegio de México, 2008.

Bolivar S., *Message to the Congress of Angostura, 1819*, http://www.fordham.edu/HALSAll/MOD/1819bolivar.asp (27.09.2012).

Camacho Roldán S., *El estudio sobre la sociolgía*, [in:] L. Zea, *Pensamiento positivista latinoamericano*, Caracas, Venezuela, Biblioteca Ayacucho, 1980.

Candia Baeza C., *Filosofía, identidad y pensamiento político en Latinoamérica*, „Polis: Revista Académica de la Universidad Bolivariana" 2008, No. 18.

Cannabrava E., *Elementos de metodologia filosófica*, São Paulo, Companhia Editora Nacional, 1956.

Cannabrava E., *Ensaios filosóficos*, Rio de Janeiro, Ministério da Educação e Cultura, Instituto Nacional do Livro, 1957.

Cannabrava E., *Present Tendencies in Latin American Philosophy*, „The Journal of Philosophy" 1949, Vol. 46, No. 5.

Cappelletti A. J., *Prólogo*, [in:] C. M. Rama, A. J. Cappelletti, *El anarquismo en América Latina*, Caracas, Venezuela, Biblioteca Ayacucho, 1990.

Carmona D., *Es fusilado Julio López, calificado de „comunista, asesino y gavillero"*, „Memoria Política de México" 9 VII 1868, www.memoriapoliticademexico.org/ Efemerides/7/09071868-JCh.html (31.01.2015).

Caso A., *Filósofos y doctrinas morales*, Mexico City, Porrúa Hermanos, 1915.

Clark M. L., *The Emergence and Transformation of Positivism*, [in:] S. Nuccetelli, O. Schutte, O. Bueno, *A Companion to Latin American Philosophy*, Malden, Massachusetts, Wiley-Blackwell, 2010 [online:] http://dx.doi. org/10.1002/9781444314847.ch4.

Comte A., Harriet M., *The Positive Philosophy*, New York, AMS Press, 1974.

Comte A., *The Positive Philosophy of Auguste Comte*, trans. H. Martineau, Vol. 3, London, G. Bell & Sons, 1896.

Coronil F., *Latin American Postcolonial Studies and Global Decolonization*, [in:] N. Lazarus, *The Cambridge Companion to Postcolonial Literary Studies*, Cambridge, Cambridge University Press, 2004 [online:] http://dx.doi.org/10.1017/ CCOL0521826942.012.

Coutinho A., *Some Considerations on the Problem of Philosophy in Brazil*, „Philosophy and Phenomenological Research" 1943, Vol. 4, No. 2.

Cruz Revueltas J. C., *La filosofía en América Latina como problema y un epílogo desde la otra orilla*, Mexico City, Publicaciones Cruz, 2003.

Dembicz A., Górski E., Malinowski M., Paradowski R., Rodriguez F., Dembicz K., *Pensamiento filosófico del CESLA*, Warsaw, CESLA UW, 2012.

Dembicz A., *Filozofia poznawania Ameryki*, Warsaw, CESLA, 2010.

Derwich K., *W krainie pierzastego węża. Historia Meksyku od podboju do czasów współczesnych*, Cracow, Universitas, 2014.

Díaz Díaz G., Santos Escudero C., *Bibliografia filosofica hispanica: 1901-1970*, Madrid, Consejo Superior de Investigaciones Cientif., Inst. de Filosofia Luis Vives, Dept. de Filosofia Española, 1982.

Dussel E. D., *Philosophy of Liberation*, Maryknoll, New York, Orbis Books, 1985.

Dussel E. D., Mendieta E., *The Underside of Modernity: Apel, Ricoeur, Rorty, Taylor, and the Philosophy of Liberation*, Atlantic Highlands, New Jersey, Humanities Press, 1996.

Dussel E. D., *Ética de la liberación en la edad de la globalización y la exclusión*, Madrid, Trotta, 1998.

Dussel E. D., *Eurocentrism and Modernity (Introduction to the Frankfurt Lectures)*, [in:] J. Beverley, M. Aronna, J. Oviedo (eds.), *The Postmodernism Debate in Latin America*, Durham, North Carolina, Duke University Press, 1995 [online:] http://dx.doi.org/10.2307/303341.

Dussel E. D., *Transmodernity and Interculturality: An Interpretation from the Perspective of Philosophy of Liberation*, „Transmodernity: Journal of Peripheral Cultural Production of the Luso-Hispanic World" 2012, Vol. 3, No. 1.

Dussel E. D., *Transmodernity and Interculturality*, „Poligrafi (International Edition)" 2006, Vol. 11, No. 41/42.

Dussel E. D., Neely A., *A History of the Church in Latin America: Colonialism to Liberation (1492-1979)*, Grand Rapids, Michigan, Wm. B. Eerdmans, 1981.

Ezcurdia M., *Originalidad y presencia*, [in:] J. C. Cruz Revueltas, *La filosofía en América Latina como problema y un epílogo desde la otra orilla*, Mexico City, Publicaciones Cruz, 2003.

Flores Magón R., Araujo A. D. P., Owen W. C., *Land and liberty: Mexico's Battle for Economic Freedom and its Relation to Labor's World-Wide Struggle*, Los Angeles, Calif., Mexican Liberal Party, 1913.

Flores Magón R., *Regeneración*, September 10, November 19, 1910, [in:] M. Rama, A. J. Cappelletti, *El anarquismo en América Latina*, Caracas, Venezuela, Biblioteca Ayacucho, 1990.

Forment G. E., *Filosofía de hispanoamérica. Aproximaciones al panorama actual*, Barcelona, ICE, University of Barcelona, 1987.

Fornet-Betancourt R., *De la significación de la filosofía latinoamericana para la superación del eurocentrismo*, „Revista de Filosofía" 2010, Vol. 65, No. 2.

Fornet-Betancourt R., *La filosofía de liberación en América Latina*, [in:] G. E. Forment, *Filosofía de hispanoamérica. Aproximaciones al panorama actual*, Barcelona, ICE, University of Barcelona, 1987.

Frondizi R., *A Study In Recent Mexican Thought*, „The Review of Metaphysics" 1955, Vol. 9, No. 1.

Frondizi R., *Is There an Ibero-American Philosophy?*, „Philosophy and Phenomenological Research" III 1949, Vol. 9, No. 3, Special Issue – Second Inter-American Congress of Philosophy.

Frondizi R., *On the Unity of the Philosophies of the Two Americas*, „The Review of Metaphysics" 1951, Vol. 4, No. 4.

Frondizi R., *Panorama de la filosofia latinoamericana contemporanea*, „Minerva" 1944, Vol. 1, No. 2.

Frondizi R., *Philosophy*, „Handbook of Latin American Studies" 1939, Vol. 6.

Frondizi R., *Tendencies in Contemporary Latin-American Philosophy*, [in:] *Inter-American Intellectual Interchange*, Austin, Institute of Latin American Studies, University of Texas, 1943.

Frondizi R., Gracia J. J. E., *Ensayos filosóficos*, Mexico City, Fondo de Cultura Económica, 1986.

Fuentes C., *Prolog to José Enrique Rodó: Ariel*, Austin, University of Texas Press, 1988.

Gaos J., *El pensamiento hispanoamericano. Antología del pensamiento de lengua española en la edad contemporánea*, Mexico City, National Autonomous University of Mexico, Coordinación de Humanidades, 1993.

García-Ramírez E., *On the Invisibility Problem of Latin American Philosophy*, „APA Newsletter on Hispanic/Latino Issues in Philosophy" 2011, Vol. 10, No. 2 (Spring), http://c.ymcdn.com/sites/www.apaonline.org/resource/collection /60044C96-F3E0-4049-BC5A-271C673FA1E5/v10n2Hispanic.pdf.

Garrido M., Orringer N. R., Valdés L. M.,Valdés M. M. (eds.), *El legado filosófico español e hispanoamericano del siglo XX*, Madrid, Cátedra, 2009.

Gilson G., *The Project of Exact Philosophy: An Interview with Mario Bunge, Frothingham Chair of Logic and Metaphysics*, „APA Newsletter on Hispanic/Latino Issues in Philosophy" 2006, Vol. 1.

Given L. M., *The Sage Encyclopedia of Qualitative Research Methods*, Los Angeles, Calif., SAGE, 2008 [online:] http://dx.doi.org/10.4135/9781412963909.

Godio J., *Historia del movimiento obrero latinoamericano*, Vol. 1, Mexico City, Nueva Sociedad, 1983.

Gracia J. J. E., *Ethnic Labels and Philosophy*, „Philosophy Today" 1999, Vol. 43, No. 4.

Gracia J. J. E., *Hispanic Philosophy: Its Beginning and Golden Age*, „The Review of Metaphysics" 1993, Vol. 46, No. 3.

Gracia J. J. E., *Identidad hispánica/latina. Una perspectiva filosófica*, Mexico City, Paidós, 2006.

Gracia J. J. E., *Identity and Latin American Philosophy*, [in:] S. Nuccetelli, O. Schutte, O. Bueno, *A Companion to Latin American Philosophy*, Malden, Massachusetts, Wiley-Blackwell, 2010.

Gracia J. J. E., *Forging People: Race, Ethnicity, and Nationality in Hispanic American and Latino/a Thought*, Notre Dame, Indiana, University of Notre Dame Press, 2011 [online:] http://dx.doi.org/10.1111/blar.12165.

Gracia J. J. E., *Hispanic Philosophy: Its Beginning and Golden Age*, „Review of Metaphysics" 1993, Vol. 46.

Gracia J. J. E., *Importance of the History of Ideas in Latin America: Zea's Positivism in Mexico*, „Journal of the History of Ideas" 1975, No. 36.

Gracia J. J. E., *Individuality, Life Plans, and Identity: Foundational Concepts in Appiah's The Ethics of Identity*, „Journal of Social Philosophy" 2006, Vol. 37, No. 2 [online:] http://dx.doi.org/10.1111/j.1467-9833.2006.00333.x.

Gracia J. J. E., *Latin American Philosophy in the Twentieth Century*, Buffalo, Prometheus Books, 1986.

Gracia J. J. E., *Latin American Philosophy Today*, „Philosophical Forum" 1988-89, Vol. 1-2.

Gracia J. J. E., *Latinos in America: Philosophy and social Identity*, Malden, Massachusetts, Blackwell Pub., 2008.

Gracia J. J. E., *Philosophical Analysis in Latin America*, „History of Philosophy Quarterly" 1984, Vol. 1, No. 1.

Gracia J. J. E., *Philosophy and Its History: Issues in Philosophical Historiography*, Albany, State University of New York Press, 1992.

Gracia J. J. E., *Philosophy and Literature in Latin America*, New York, State University of New York Press, 1989.

Gracia J. J. E., *Race, Ethnicity, and Nationality: A Challenge for the 21st Century*, Lanham, Maryland, Rowman & Littlefield, 2005.

Gracia J. J. E., *What is Latin American Philosophy?*, [in:] G. Yancy, *Philosophy in Multiple Voices*, Lanham, Maryland, Rowman & Littlefield Publishers, 2007.

Gracia J. J. E., Jaksić I., *Filosofía e identidad cultural en América Latina*, Caracas, Venezuela, Monte Avila Editores, 1988.

Gracia J. J. E., Jaksić I., *Introduction*, Part 3, [in:] J. J. E. Gracia, *Latin American Philosophy in the Twentieth Century*, Buffalo, Prometheus Books, 1986.

Gracia J. J. E, Millán-Zaibert E., *Latin American Philosophy for the 21st Century: The Human Condition, Values, and the Search for Identity*, Amherst, New York, Prometheus Books, 2004.

Gracia J. J. E., Rabossi E., Villanueva E., Dascal M. (eds.), *Philosophical Analysis in Latin America*, Dordrecht, Holland, D. Reidel Pub. Co., 1984 [online:] http://dx.doi.org/10.1002/9780470696484.

Grušovnik, T., *A Distant View: Globalization Inside Philosophy*, „Synthesis Philosophica" 2009, Vol. 24, No. 1.

Guerrer P., *Regeneración*, September 10, 1910, [in:] C. M. Rama, A. J. Cappelletti, *El anarquismo en América Latina*, Caracas, Venezuela, Biblioteca Ayacucho, 1990.

Guttiérrez G., *Las Casas: In Search of the Poor Jesus Christ*, Maryknoll, New York, Orbis, 1993.

Hart J. M., *Anarchism & the Mexica Working Class, 1860-1931*, Austin, University of Texas Press, 1978.

Horváth G., Szabó S., *El positivismo en Brasil y México. Un estudio comparativo*, „Tzintzun. Revista de Estudios Históricos" 2005, No. 42.

Hountondji P. J., *Scientific Dependence in Africa Today*, „Research in African Literatures" 1990, Vol. 21, No. 3.

Hurtado G., *Two Models of Latin American Philosophy*, „Journal of Speculative Philosophy" 2006, Vol. 20, No. 3.

Hurtado G., *El búho y la serpiente. Ensayos sobre la filosofía en México en el siglo XX*, Mexico City, UNAM, 2007.

Hurtado G., *El diálogo filosófico interamericano como un diálogo para la democracia*, „Inter-American Journal of Philosophy" 2010, Vol. 1, No. 1.

Iannone P., *Dictionary of World Philosophy*, New York, Routledge, 2001.

Iannone P. (ed.), *Latin American Philosophy*, [in:] idem, *Dictionary of World Philosophy*, New York, Routledge, 2001.

Illades C., *Rhodakanaty y la formación del pensamiento socialista en México*, „Revista Europea de Estudios Latinoamericanos y del Caribe" IX 2004, No. 77.

Illades C., *Rhodakanaty y la formación del pensamiento socialista en México, Rubí*, Barcelona, Anthropos Editorial, 2002.

Ingenieros J., *La evolución de las ideas argentinas*, „Revista de la Universidad de Buenos Aires" 1914, Vol. 27; page reference is to Buenos Aires, ed. by L. J. Rosso, 1937.

Ingenieros J., *Educación, escuela, maestro*, [in:] L. Zea, *Pensamiento positivista latinoamericano*, Caracas, Venezuela, Biblioteca Ayacucho, 1980.

Inglehart R., Carballo M., *Does Latin America Exist? (And is There a Confucian Culture?): A Global Analysis of Cross-Cultural Differences*, „PS: Political Science & Politics" 1997, Vol. 30, No. 1.

Irvine A. B., *An Ontological Critique of the Trans-Ontology of Enrique Dussel*, „Sophia: International Journal for Philosophy of Religion, Metaphysical Theology and Ethics" 2011, Vol. 50, No. 4.

Isasi-Díaz A. M., Mendieta E., *Decolonizing Epistemologies Latina/o Theology and Philosophy*, New York, Fordham University Press, 2012.

Jorrín M., Martz J. D., *Latin American Political Thought and Ideology*, Chapel Hill, University of North Carolina Press, 1970.

Kłosowicz R., *Documents and Readings in American History: From the Colonies to the End of the Nineteenth Century*, Cracow, WUJ, 2005.

Krusé C., *The Third Inter-American Congress of Philosophy*, „The Journal of Philosophy" 1950, Vol. 47, No. 12.

Kuhn Th. S., *The Structure of Scientific Revolutions*, 3rd ed., Chicago, University of Chicago Press, 1996.

Kuklick B., *A History of Philosophy in America, 1720-2000*, Oxford, Clarendon Press, 2001.

Lagarrigue J., *Positivismo y catolicismo*, [in:] L. Zea, *Pensamiento positivista latino-americano*, Caracas, Venezuela, Biblioteca Ayacucho, 1980.

Las Casas B. de, *Bartolomé de las Casas: The Only Way*, H. R. Parish (ed.), Mahwah, New Jersey, Paulist Press, 1992.

Lastarria J. V., *The Latin-American Mind*, trans. L. Zea, Norman, University of Oklahoma Press, 1963.

Lazarus N., *The Cambridge Companion to Postcolonial Literary Studies*, Cambridge, Cambridge University Press, 2004 [online:] http://dx.doi.org/10.1002/9780470696484.

León-Portilla M., *Aztec Thought and Culture*, Norman, University of Oklahoma Press, 1963.

Leroy C., *Los secretos del anarquismo. Prólogo de E. Guardiola y Cardellac*, Mexico City, Libreria Renacimiento, 1913.

Martí O. R., *Early Critics of Positivism*, [in:] S. Nuccetelli, O. Schutte, O. Bueno, *A Companion to Latin American Philosophy*, Malden, Massachusetts, Wiley-Blackwell, 2010.

Martí O. R., *Is There a Latin American Philosophy*, „Metaphilosophy" 1983, Vol. 14, No. 1.

Mattelart A., Siegelaub S., *Communication and Class Struggle: An Anthology in 2 Volumes*, Vol. 1, New York, International General, 1979.

Mendieta E., *Latin American Philosophy: Currents, Issues, Debates*, Bloomington, IN, Indiana University Press, 2003.

Mignolo W., *The Idea of Latin America*, Malden, Massachusetts, Blackwell Pub., 2005.

Mill J. S, *Collected Works of John Stuart Mill*, Vol. 32, Toronto, University of Toronto Press, 1991.

Millán-Zaibert E., *A Great Vanishing Act?: The Latin American Philosophical Tradition and How Ariel and Caliban Helped Save It from Oblivion*, „CR: The New Centennial Review" 2008, Vol. 7, No. 3.

Miró Quesada F., *El problema de la filosofía latinoamericana*, Mexico City, Fondo de Cultura Económica, 1976.

Montiel E., *Three Decisive Battles for Latin American Philosophy*, „Cultura: New Dimensions of Music, Literature and Philosophy" 1982, Vol. 8, No. 2.

Moraña M., Dussel E. D., Jáuregui C. A., *Coloniality at Large: Latin America and the Postcolonial Debate*, Durham, Duke University Press, 2008.

Nettlau M., *Actividad anarquista en México. Rhodakanaty y Zalacosta. Ricardo Flores Magón, Regeneración y las insurrecciones por 'tierra y libertad'. Apuntes sobre la propaganda anarquista y sindical tardía*, Mexico City, Federal District, Instituto Nacional de Antropología e Historia, 2008.

Nuccetelli S., *Is „Latin-American Thought" Philosophy*, „Methaphilosophy" 2003, Vol. 34, No. 4 (July).

Nuccetelli S., *Latin American Ethics*, [in:] *International Encyclopedia of Ethics*, H. LaFollette (ed.), Cambridge, Massachusetts, Wiley-Blackwell, 2013.

Nuccetelli S., *Latin American Philosophy: Metaphilosophical Foundations*, [in:] *The Stanford Encyclopedia of Philosophy*, (Fall 2013 Edition), E. N. Zalta (ed.), http://plato.stanford.edu/archives/sum2014/entries/latin-american-metaphilosophy/, http://plato.stanford.edu/archives/fall2013/entries/latin-american-philosophy/ (01.09.2015).

Nuccetelli S., *Latin American Philosophy: Metaphilosophical Foundations*, [in:] *The Stanford Encyclopedia of Philosophy*, (Summer 2014 Edition), E. N. Zalta (ed.), http://plato.stanford.edu/archives/sum2014/entries/latin-american-metaphilosophy/ (01.09.2015).

Nuccetelli S., *Latin American Thought: Philosophical Problems and Arguments*, Boulder, Colorado, Westview Press, 2002.

Nuccetelli S., Schutte O., Bue O., *A Companion to Latin American Philosophy*, Malden, Massachusetts, Wiley-Blackwell, 2010.

Nuñez R., *La reforma politica en Colombia*, [in:] L. Zea, *Pensamiento positivista latinoamericano*, Caracas, Venezuela, Biblioteca Ayacucho, 1980.

Olsson M. R., *Postmodernism*, [in:] L. M. Given, *The Sage Encyclopedia of Qualitative Research Methods*, Los Angeles, Calif., SAGE, 2008.

Pappas G. F., *Pragmatism in the Americas*, New York, Fordham University Press, 2011.

Pappas G. G., *El punto de partida de la filosofía en Risieri Frondizi y el pragmatism*, „Anuario Filosófico" 2007, Vol. 40, No. 2.

Pereda C., *Latin American Philosophy: Some Vices*, „Journal of Speculative Philosophy" 2006, Vol. 20, No. 3.

Phaf-Rheinberger I., *Myths of Early Modernity: Historical and Contemporary Narratives on Brazil and Angola*, „CR: The New Centennial Review" 2008, Vol. 7, No. 3.

Pickering M., *Auguste Comte: An Intellectual Biography*, Cambridge, Cambridge University Press, 1993.

Pickering M., *Auguste Comte: An Intellectual Biography*, Vol. 3, Cambridge, CUP, 2009.

Potter J., *Discourse Analysis*, [in:] L. M. Given, *The Sage Encyclopedia of Qualitative Research Methods*, Los Angeles, Calif., SAGE, 2008.

Raat W. D., *Los intelectuales, el positivismo y la cuestión indígena*, „Historia Mexicana" 1971, Vol. 20, No. 3.

Rabossi E., *Latin American Philosophy*, [in:] Th. Baldwin, *The Cambridge History of Philosophy*, 1870-1945, Cambridge, UK, Cambridge University Press, 2003.

Rabossi E., *En el comienzo Dios creo el Canon. Biblia berolinensis. Ensayos sobre la condición de la filosofía*, Buenos Aires, Gedisa, 2008.

Rabossi E., *Filosofar. Profesionalismo, profesionalidad, tics y modales*, [in:] J. C. Cruz Revueltas (ed.), *La filosofía en América Latina como problema y un epílogo desde la otra orilla*, Mexico City, Publicaciones Cruz, 2003.

Rama C. M., Cappelletti A. J., *El anarquismo en América Latina*, Caracas, Venezuela, Biblioteca Ayacucho, 1990.

Redmont W., *Self-awareness in Latin-American Colonial Philosophy*, Part 1, „Jahrbuch für Geschichte Lateinamerikas" 2004, No. 41 and Part 2, „Jahrbuch für Geschichte Lateinamerikas" 2005, No. 42.

Rhodakanaty P. C., *Programa social-último sacrificio. Dererminación del nivel histórico*, „El Socialista" V 1876, No. 178.

Ribera C. A., *La Casa del Obrero Mundial. Anarcosindicalismo y revolución en México*, Mexico City, Federal District, Instituto Nacional de Antropología e Historia, 2010.

Richard N., *Postmodernism and Periphery*, „Third Text" 1987/1988, No. 2.

Riley I. W., *American Philosophy, the Early Schools*, New York, Dodd Mead, 1907.

Sánchez Reulet A., *Contemporary Latin-American Philosophy: A Selection, with an Introduction and Notes*, Albuquerque, University of New Mexico Press, 1954.

Riuz-Aho E., *Latin American Philosophy at a Crossroads*, „Human Studies" 2011, Vol. 34, No. 3 [online:] http://dx.doi.org/10.1002/9780470696484.

Roig A., *Teoría y crítica del pensamiento latinoamericano*, Mexico City, Fondo de Cultura Económica, 1981.

Roig A. (ed.), *El pensamiento social y político iberoamericano del siglo XIX*, Vol. 22, „Enciclopedia Iberoamericana de Filosofia", Madrid, Editorial Trotta, 2000.

Romero F., *Filosofía de la persona y otros ensayos*, Buenos Aires, Losada, 1944.

Romero F., *Tendencias contemporáneas en el pensamiento hispanoamericano*, „Philosophy and Phenomenological Research" 1943, Vol. 4, No. 2.

Romero J. L., Velen V. A., *Latin America and the Idea of Europe*, „Diogenes" 1964, Vol. 12, No. 47.

Salazar Bondy A., *The Meaning and Problem of Hispanic American Thought*, Lawrence, Center of Latin American Studies of the University of Kansas, 1969.

Santos Herceg J., *Filosofía de (para) la Conquista. Eurocentrismo y colonialismo en la disputa por el Nuevo Mundo*, „Atenea (Concepción)" 2011, No. 503 [online:] http://dx.doi.org/10.4067/S0718-04622011000100009.

Sarmineto D. F., *Agripolis o la capital de los estados confederados del Rio de la Plata*, [in:] L. Zea, *Pensamiento positivista latinoamericano*, Caracas, Venezuela, Biblioteca Ayacucho, 1980.

Schiller H. I., *Communication and Cultural Domination*, White Plains, New York, International Arts and Sciences Press, 1976.

Schutte O., *Cultural Identity and Social Liberation in Latin American Thought*, Albany, State University of New York Press, 1993.

Schutte O., Resistance to Colonialism: Latin American Legacies, University of Chicago Conference: Colonialism and Its Legacies (Conference Draft 4-04; Subject to Further Revision), University of South Florida, 2004, http://icspt. uchicago.edu/papers/2004/schutte04.pdf (12.03.2013).

Seed P., *Colonial and Postcolonial Discourse*, [Review of *Colonial Encounters: Europe and the Native Caribbean, 1492-1797; Discursos narrativos de la Conquista: Mitificacion y emergencia; Unfinished Conversations: Mayas and Foreigners Between Two Wars; Contracting Colonialism: Translation and Christian Conversion in Tagalog Society Under Early Spanish Rule; Pasyon and Revolution: Popular Movements in the Philippines, 1840-1910*], „Latin American Research Review" 1991, Vol. 26, No. 3.

Sierra J., *Iniciativa para crear la universidad*, [in:] L. Zea, *Pensamiento positivista latinoamericano*, Caracas, Venezuela, Biblioteca Ayacucho, 1980.

Sierra J., *Sobre política nacional*, [in:] L. Zea, *Pensamiento positivista latinoamericano*, Caracas, Venezuela, Biblioteca Ayacucho, 1980.

Spencer H., *Essays: Scientific, Political and Speculative*, Vol. 1, London, Williams & Norgate, 1891.

Spencer H., *Principles of Biology*, Vol. 1, London, Williams & Norgate, 1864.

Spencer H., *Social Statics or the Conditions Essential to Happiness Specified and the First of them Developed*, London, John Chapman, 1851.

Sturm F. G., *Dependence and Originality in Iberoamerican Philosophy*, „International Philosophical Quarterly" 1980, Vol. 20, No. 3.

Swanson Ph., *The Companion to Latin American Studies*, London, Arnold, 2003.

Tisdell E. J., *Feminist Epistemology*, [in:] L. M. Given, *The Sage Encyclopedia of Qualitative Research Methods*, Los Angeles, Calif., SAGE, 2008.

Tomlinson J., *Cultural Imperialism: A Critical Introduction*, Baltimore, Maryland, Johns Hopkins University Press, 1991.

Vargas M., *On the Value of Philosophy: The Latin American Case*, „Comparative Philosophy" 2010, Vol. 1, No. 1.

Vargas M., *„Real" Philosophy, Metaphilosophy, and Metametaphilosophy: On the Plight of Latin American Philosophy*, „CR: The New Centennial Review" 2007, Vol. 7, No. 3 (Winter).

Vega I. G. de la, *O Inkach uwagi prawdziwe*, Warsaw, CESLA, 2000 (Comentarios reales de los Incas).

Velásquez García E., *Nueva historia general de México*, Mexico City, Colegio de México, 2011.

Yancy G., *Philosophy in Multiple Voices*, Lanham, Rowman & Littlefield Publishers, 2007.

Young R. A., *Latin American Postmodernisms*, Amsterdam, Rodopi, 1997.

Young R. A., *Postcolonialism*, Oxford, Oxford University Press, 2003.

Zea L., *Del liberalismo a la revolución en la educación mexicana*, Mexico City, Talleres Gráficos de la Nación, 1956.

Zea L., *En torno a una filosofia americana*, „Cuadernos Americanos" 1942, Vol. 3, No. 3.

Zea L., *Identity: A Latin American Philosophical Problem*, „Philosophical Forum" 1988-1989, Vol. 20, No. 1-2 (Fall-Winter).

Zea L., *Philosophy and Thought in Latin America*, „Latin American Research Review" 1968, Vol. 3, No. 2 (Spring).

Zea L., *The Actual Function of Philosophy in Latin America*, [in:] J. J. E Gracia, E. Millán-Zaibert, *Latin American Philosophy for the 21st Century: The Human Condition, Values, and the Search for Identity*, Amherst, New York, Prometheus Books, 2004.


*Declaration of Independence*, July 4, 1776, [in:] R. Kłosowicz, *Documents and Readings in American History: From the Colonies to the End of the Nineteenth Century*, Cracow, WUJ, 2005.

*Manifiesto Anarquista del Grupo Luz*, [in:] C. A. Ribera, *La Casa del Obrero Mundial. Anarcosindicalismo y revolución en México*, Mexico City, Federal District, Instituto Nacional de Antropología e Historia, 2010.

*Manifesto del Partido Liberal Mexicano*, September 23, 1911, [in:] M. Rama, A. J. Cappelletti, *El anarquismo en América Latina*, Caracas, Venezuela, Biblioteca Ayacucho, 1990.

*Programa del Partido Liberal y Manifesto a la Nación, 1 de Julio 1906*, [in:] M. Rama, A. J. Cappelletti, *El anarquismo en América Latina*, Caracas, Venezuela, Biblioteca Ayacucho, 1990.